German Short Stories
9 Simple and Captivating Stories for Effective German Learning for Beginners

© **Copyright 2018**

All rights Reserved. No part of this book may be reproduced in any form without permission in writing from the author. Reviewers may quote brief passages in reviews.

Disclaimer: No part of this publication may be reproduced or transmitted in any form or by any means, mechanical or electronic, including photocopying or recording, or by any information storage and retrieval system, or transmitted by email without permission in writing from the publisher.

While all attempts have been made to verify the information provided in this publication, neither the author nor the publisher assumes any responsibility for errors, omissions or contrary interpretations of the subject matter herein.

This book is for entertainment purposes only. The views expressed are those of the author alone, and should not be taken as expert instruction or commands. The reader is responsible for his or her own actions.

Adherence to all applicable laws and regulations, including international, federal, state and local laws governing professional licensing, business practices, advertising and all other aspects of doing business in the US, Canada, UK or any other jurisdiction is the sole responsibility of the purchaser or reader.

Neither the author nor the publisher assumes any responsibility or liability whatsoever on the behalf of the purchaser or reader of these materials. Any perceived slight of any individual or organization is purely unintentional.

Contents

INTRODUCTION 1

CHAPTER 1 – HOW TO READ EFFECTIVELY 3

CHAPTER 2 – DER MANN UND DAS PFERD (THE MAN AND THE HORSE) 6

CHAPTER 3 – DER TOTE SAMEN (THE DEAD SEED) 15

CHAPTER 4 – EIN WAHRER FREUND (A TRUE FRIEND) 25

CHAPTER 5 – SCHALEN AUS HOLZ (WOODEN BOWLS)...................32

CHAPTER 6 – EINE BRÜCKE DES FRIEDENS (A PEACEFUL BRIDGE) 39

CHAPTER 7 – DU BIST WAS DU DENKST (YOU ARE WHAT YOU THINK)..47

CHAPTER 8 – DER TAXIFAHRER (THE TAXI DRIVER) 54

CHAPTER 9 – JULIA RETTET DEN KINDERGARTEN (JULIA SAVES THE KINDERGARTEN)..64

CHAPTER 10 – EIN WAHRER HELD (A TRUE HERO)..........................75

CONCLUSION...86

    PREVIEW OF GERMAN 88
    AN ESSENTIAL GUIDE TO GERMAN LANGUAGE LEARNING.................................. 88

INTRODUCTION 88

CHAPTER 1 – PRONUNCIATION...90

    LEARNING THE GERMAN ALPHABET 90
    DIPHTHONGS 92
    THE "SCH" AND "CH"... 93
    LETTER CASE 94
    SUMMARY 94
    EXERCISES 94

CHAPTER 2 – THE BASICS 96
NOUNS - MAIN WORDS 96

Introduction

How do you learn to write well? How do you expand your vocabulary? How can you improve your ability to express your thoughts and ideas? How can you improve your foreign language skills in a pleasant and varied way? A reasonable way is undoubtedly: to read as much as possible! For this reason, we warmly recommend that you read the stories in this book if you want to learn more words and improve your verbal or written expression. We made it easy for you to read these interesting stories by simply offering a translation in English. You can learn some new words and answer questions about them at the end. This is a way to learn German and still have fun.

Through regular reading you get a feeling for the foreign language and for the sentence structure and you can see how vocabulary is used in the context and get to know lots of new words. Do not be confused by unknown structures. Just read - you do not read to study grammar, but to read with pleasure, right? In the beginning, it is certainly better to try to understand the story in German, but if you need some help, you have everything you need in English. So start with small steps and work your way through slowly. But the most important step is: just start and read regularly, preferably every day.

The advantages of reading are obvious. Reading broadens the human horizon, enriching its inner world, making it more intelligent, and positively impacting memory. It is also important to read because reading expands the vocabulary and promotes the development of clearer thinking, which allows one to clearly formulate and express thoughts. It will definitely help you to express yourself and choose the right words. This is why you should take a look at the stories we have for you. Try to read them and just have fun!

Chapter 1 – How to read effectively

Effective reading is not about being as fast as possible, but about understanding the content and keeping it in mind. To understand when effective reading is especially helpful, two different ways of reading must be distinguished:

Pleasure. Of course, when you're reading for yourself, effectiveness is not the first thing you think about. Nevertheless, it can increase your reading pleasure. Effective reading can help you appreciate your book even more through better understanding.

Learning. Anyone who has ever had to read several books for an exam knows how valuable and helpful effective reading can be. It saves time, energy, and in the case of learning, it can make everything easier.

When reading the stories, enjoyment and a sense of achievement are vitally important because that keeps you coming back for more. The more you read, the more you learn. The best way to enjoy reading and to feel that sense of achievement is by reading entire chapters from beginning to end. Consequently, reaching the end of a book is the most important thing ... more important than understanding every word in it! And this brings us to the single most important point: You don't need to understand everything you read. This is completely normal and to be expected. The fact that you do not know a word or phrase does not mean that you're "stupid" or "not good enough." It simply means you're engaged in the language learning process, just like everybody else.

So what should you do when there's something you do not understand? Sooner or later you can get to a point where you don't understand something. A foreign word, a concept or a phrase - nobody knows everything. Therefore, take the time to look up these things to really understand it. The same applies if, for example, in context people or places are mentioned which you can not assign to something. The more accurate your information, the better you will understand the content. If you find yourself stumped by an unknown word, here are five ways to tackle the problem:

Look at the word and see if it's familiar in any way. Take a guess - you might surprise yourself! Go back and read the word a few times. Using the context of that sentence, and everything else that's happening in the story, try to guess what the unknown word might mean. This takes practice, but is often easier than you think! If you can't find the word in the translation or in the vocabulary list, write the word down and find the meaning later. Then keep reading.

Sometimes, you might find a word that is in the past tense or that looks unfamiliar. For example:

Wohnte (inf. Wohnen) – lived (live)

Nahm (inf. nehmen) – took (take)

Kam (inf. Kommen) – came (come)

You may not recognize the word at first, but you can look at the whole sentence and see if something would make sense. You may get it on your own. Don't be frustrated.

Stages of learning to read a text:

Learn to recognize individual words and phrases.

Try to understand the meaning of the sentence by looking at the translation.

Learn to read simple sentences, looking up words when necessary.

Learn to understand a complex text with occasional reference to a dictionary.

The key factors to your success are:

A passionate obsession for your target language and the work you want to read.

A love for learning (languages).

An understanding of how to learn, including language methods and progress tracking.

Most language learners can't enjoy reading because they think of every single word, "Why does the word have this ending?", "Why is this time used?", "Why are these subjunctive forms used all the time?", "Why is this word now actually behind this and not before?". Free yourself from wanting to analyze everything. If you're reading, it's all about understanding the text. If you want to do grammatical analysis, you have other materials at your disposal. Your brain can not concentrate on ten thought processes at the same time. You are so "killing" the fun.

One of the best ways to approach reading correctly is the "double reading method." With this method, you read the story completely, without thinking whether you have understood the text now or not. Then you try to summarize the text. Try to fix your brain on the most important points that caused the most emotions in the chapter. Then you read the chapter again and realize that it has become easier to understand the full text. This time, you can also focus more on the details and be more emotionally connected to the characters in the story.

With time, you'll see that you understand each story better. Don't force yourself and don't give up. We hope that you'll enjoy these wonderful stories below!

Chapter 2 – Der Mann und das Pferd (The man and the horse)

Es war einmal ein armer Mann, der in einem **Dorf** wohnte. Dieser Mann war sehr arm, aber er besaß ein **Pferd**, das so exquisit war, das selbst **Könige** es ihm abkaufen wollten- und das zu jedem Preis. Doch der Mann lehnte immer wieder ab. Plötzlich eines Morgens, stellte er fest, dass das Pferd verschwunden war. Alle Menschen aus dem Dorf versammelten um ihr **Mitgefühl** auszudrücken.

Once upon a time there was a poor man living in a village. This man was very poor, but he owned a horse so exquisite that even kings wanted to buy it from him, at any price. But the man refused, again and again. But suddenly, one morning he realized that the horse had disappeared. All the people from the village gathered to express their empathy.

Sie sagten: "Oh, was für ein **Unglück**, was hättest du für ein **Vermögen** mit diesem Pferd verdienen können und man hat dir so viel dafür geboten! Aber du warst zu **dickköpfig** und zu dumm. Jetzt ist das Pferd weg. "

They said, "Oh, what a misfortune, you have earned a fortune with this horse and you were offered so much for it, but unfortunately you were too stubborn and too stupid, now the horse is gone."

Aber der alte Mann lachte nur und sagte: "Ach redet doch keinen **Unsinn**: "Alles was man darüber sagen kann, ist, dass das Pferd jetzt nicht mehr in seinem **Stall** ist. Lass die **Zukunft** kommen und uns zeigen was passiert"

But the old man just laughed and said, "Oh, do not talk nonsense. All that can be said now is that the horse is no longer in his stable. Let the future come and show us what happens.

Nach wenigen Tagen kehrte das Pferd plötzlich zurück in seinen Stall. Nichticht nur das, es brachte eine ganze Herde wilder Pferde aus dem Wald mit. Und wieder versamelte sich das ganze Dorf und sie sagten: "Unglaublich, der alte Mann hatte **Recht** sein Pferd ist tatsächlich zurückgekommen, und es hat auch noch ein ganzes **dutzend** toller Pferde mitgebracht. Jetzt kann er so viel Geld verdienen, wie er will." Und sie gingen zu dem alten Mann und sagten: "Oh es tut uns Leid wir konnten das ja nicht voraussehen und die Wege Gottes verstehen, aber du bist unglaublich. Du hast es wohl irgendwie geahnt. Vielleicht kannst du sogar die Zukunft voraussehen."

And then, after a few days, the horse suddenly returned to his stable. And not only that, it brought a whole herd of wild horses out of the forest. And again, the whole village gathered and they said, "Unbelievable, the old man was right, his horse has actually come back, and it has brought back a dozen great horses and now he can make as much money as he wants." And they went to the old man and said, "Oh, sorry, we could not foresee that and understand the ways of God, but you are incredible, you probably guessed, maybe you can even foretell the future."

"So ein **Quatsch**." sagte der alte Mann nur. "Ich weiß nur, eins: Nämlich, dass das Pferd mit einer ganzen Herde Pferde zurückgekommen ist und was morgen geschehen wird, das weiß nur der liebe Gott."

"That's crap," said the old man. "All I know is one thing: the fact that the horse came back with a whole herd of horses and what will happen tomorrow, only God knows."

Und schon ein paar Tage später geschah es, das der einzige Sohn des Mannes, der die neuen Pferde zu **reiten** wollte, dabei vom Pferd fiel. Er **brach** sich dabei seine Beine so schwer, das er fortan wohl nicht mehr würde richtig laufen können. Die Menschen kamen wieder zu dem alten Mann und sagten: "Du hast recht gehabt. Man weiß nie. Die Sache mit den Pferden hat sich als ein **Fluch** erwiesen. Da wäre es besser gewesen, wären die Pferde überhaupt gar nicht erst gekommen. Nun wird dein Sohn für sein ganzes Leben lang **verkrüppelt** sein.

And a few days later, the only son of the man who wanted to ride the new horses fell off his horse. He broke his legs so hard that he could no longer walk properly. People came back to the old man and said, "You were right, you never know, the horse thing turned out to be a curse, so he would have been better if the horses did not return at all. Your son will be crippled for life now.

Aber der alte Mann sagte wieder nur: "Nicht so voreilig. Wartet ab! Man wird sehen was geschieht. Man kann nämlich nur eines darüber sagen, nämlich, dass mein Sohn sich die Beine gebrochen hat. Das ist alles."

But the old man said again, "Don't be to hasty, wait, you'll see what happens, you can only say one thing about it, that my son broke his leg, that's all."

Einige Wochen später ergab es sich das in dem Land ein **Krieg** ausbrach und alle die jungen Männer des Dorfes von der Regierung zwangsweise eingezogen wurden. Nur der Sohn des alten Mannes durfte zu Hause bleiben, weil er für den Krieg **untauglich** war.

A few weeks later, a war broke out in the country and all the village's young men were forcibly conscripted by the government.

Only the son of the old man was allowed to stay at home because he was not able to participate.

Und wieder versammelten sich alle Menschen des Dorfes und klagten: "Unsere Söhne sind fort und du hast wenigstens noch deinen Sohn. Er mag zwar seine Beine gebrochen haben, aber er ist bei dir. Unsere Söhne sind fort und der **Feind** ist vielleicht viel mächtiger. Wahrscheinlich werden sie alle sterben. Jetzt werden wir niemanden haben, der sich im Alter um uns kümmert. Aber du hast ja noch deinen Sohn. Er wird bestimmt wieder gesund.

And again all the people of the village gathered and complained, "Our sons are gone, and you have at least your son, he may have broken his leg, but he is with you. Our sons are gone, and the enemy is perhaps much more powerful. Probably they will all die, now we will not have anyone to take care of us in old age, but you still have your son, he's sure to be well again.

Doch der alte Mann sagte wieder nur: "Man kann darüber nur eins sagen: Eure Söhne wurden eingezogen. Mein Sohn ist hier geblieben. Daraus folgt jedoch gar nichts.

But the old man said again: "One can only say one thing about this: your sons were drafted in. My son stayed here, but that does not mean anything."

Zusammenfassung

Ein alter Mann lebte in einem Dorf mit seinem Sohn und hatte ein Pferd. Das Pferd ist eines Tages verschwunden und alle Bewohner haben dem Mann gesagt, dass es besser gewesen wäre, wenn er das Pferd verkauft hätte. Der Mann hörte aber nicht darauf und beklagte sich nicht. Danach kam das Pferd wieder zurück und brachte andere Pferde auf dem Wald mit . Nach ein paar Tagen fiel sein Sohn von einem Pferd und brach sich beide Beine. Die Menschen beurteilten wieder die Situation des Mannes, aber der alte Man hörte wieder nicht darauf. Am Ende brach ein Krieg aus und alle jungen Männer, außer dem Sohn des Mannes, mussten in den Krieg gehen. Wieder kammen die Bewohner zum alten Mann und sprachen darüber wie glücklich er ist, dass sein Sohn zu Hause ist und ihre Kinder im Krieg. Der alte Mann wollte aber nicht viel darüber sprechen, denn man weiß nie, was am nächsten Tag passieren wird.

Summary

An old man lived in a village with his son and had a horse. The horse disappeared one day and all the inhabitants told the man that it would have been better if he had sold the horse. The man does not listen to it and does not complain. Then the horse comes back and brings other horses from the woods. After a few days, his son fell off a horse and broke both his legs. People again judge the man's situation, but the old man does not listen to it. In the end, a war breaks out and all young men, except the son of the man, have to go to war. Again the inhabitants come to the old man and talk about how happy he is, that his son is at home and their children are in a war. The old man does not want to talk much about it, because you never know what will happen the next day.

Wortschatz (Vocabulary)

Dorf - village

Pferd - horse

Könige - kings

Mitgefühl - empathy

Unglück – bad luck

Vermögen - fortune

Dickköpfig - stubborn

Unsinn - nonsense

Stall - stable

Zukunft - future

Recht - right (eg. Human rights)

Dutzend - dozen

Quatsch - crap

Reiten - ride

Fluch - curse

Verkrüppelt - crippled

Krieg - war

Untauglich - disabled

Feind - enemy

Fragen

1. Wie viele Pferde hatte der Mann am Anfang?

2. Mit wem lebte der Mann?

3. Wer kam immer zu dem Mann, um seine Situation zu beurteilen?

4. Was geschach als das Pferd wieder kam?

5. Was passierte mit dem Sohn des Mannes?

6. Was sagen die Bewohner des Dorfes über die Pferde, nachdem sich der Sohn verletzt hat?

a. dass es sich als ein Segen erwiesen hat

b. dass es sich als ein Fluch erwiesen hat

c. es ist einfach sein Schicksal

7. Wie viele Pferde kamen mit dem Pferd des Mannes zurück?

a. zwei

b. zehn

c. ein dutzend

8. Was hat der Sohn gebrochen als er vom Pferd fiel?

a. die Arme

b. beide Beine

c. einen Finger

9. Was sagen die Bewohner, nachdem das Pferd wieder zurück ist?

a. es ist ein magisches Pferd

b. die Pferde sind wunderschön

c. der Mann kann die Zukunft voraussehen

10. Wie endet die Geschichte?

a. die Bewohner klauen das Pferd von dem Mann

b. die Söhne der Bewohner müssen in den Krieg, während der Sohn des Mannes es nicht muss

c. der Mann zieht mit seinem Sohn in ein anderes Dorf und schenkt die Pferde den Bewohnern des Dorfes

Questions

1. How many horses did the man have in the beginning?

2. Who did the man live with?

3. Who would always come to the man to judge his situation?

4. What happened when the horse came back?

5. What happened to the son of the man?

6. What do the villagers say about the horses after their son has been injured?

a. that it turned out to be a blessing

b. that it turned out to be a curse

c. that it's just fate

7. How many horses came back with the man's horse?

a. two

b. ten

c. a dozen

8. What did the son break when he fell off his horse?

a. his arms

b. both legs

c. a finger

9. What do the inhabitants say after the horse returns?

a. it is a magical horse

b. the horses are beautiful

c. the man can foresee the future

10. How does the story end?

a. the inhabitants steal the horse from the man

b. the sons of the inhabitants must go to war, while the son of the man does not have to

c. the man moves with his son to another village and gives the horses to the inhabitants of the village

Antworten

1. Der Mann hatte ein Pferd.

2. Mit seinem Sohn.

3. Die Bewohner aus dem Dorf.

4. Das Pferd kam wieder mit einem Dutzend anderer Pferde.

5. Der Sohn des Mannes fiel vom Pferd.

6. b

7. c

8. b

9. c

10. b

Answers

1. The man had one horse.

2. With his son.

3. The inhabitants of the village.

4. The horse came back with a dozen other horses.

5. The son of the man fell off the horse.

6. b

7. c

8. b

9. c

10. b

Chapter 3 – Der tote Samen (The dead seed)

Ein erfolgreicher **Geschäftsmann** wurde älter und erkannte, dass jemand ihn ersetzen sollte. Anstatt einige seiner Kollegen oder jemanden aus seiner Familie auszuwählen, entschied er sich, etwas Ungewöhnliches zu tun. Er lud alle potenziellen Kandidaten, Finanzdirektoren, Abteilungsleiter, Kassierer, Berater, ein und gab ihnen die folgende Rede:

One successful businessman was getting older and realized that someone should replace him. Instead of choosing some of his colleagues or someone from his family, he decided to do something unusual. He invited all potential candidates, financial directors, chiefs of departments, cashiers, and advisors and gave them the following speech:

"Liebe Freunde, es ist Zeit für mich, mein Geschäft zu beenden und in einen verdienten **Ruhestand** zu gehen. Außerdem ist es jetzt die beste Zeit, einen neuen **Geschäftsführer** auszuwählen, der unser Unternehmen in Zukunft leiten wird ... Ich habe mich entschieden, dass es einer von euch sein wird. "

"Dear friends, it's time for me to finish my business and go to a deserved retirement. Also, now is the best time to choose a new general manager who will lead our company in the future. I decided that it would be one of you. "

Die jungen potenziellen Chefs waren verwirrt ...

The young prospective bosses were confused ...

"Ich werde jedem von euch einen **Samen** geben. Dies ist ein ganz besonderer Samen. Ich will, dass ihr ihn alle pflanzt und **gießt,** und nächstes Jahr wieder zurückbringt, um zu sehen, was ihr damit gemacht habt. Dann werde ich entscheiden, wer der neue Geschäftsführer sein wird. "

"I will give each of you one seed. This is a very special seed. I want all of you to plant it and water it and we will gather again next year to see what you did with it. Then I will decide who will be the new manager. "

Jim war auch bei diesem **Treffen** dabei, und wie auch alle anderen die anwesend waren, bekam er einen Samen. Als er nach Hause kam, teilte er die Nachricht mit seiner Frau und sie beschlossen, den Samen zu nähren, aus dem die **Pflanze** wachsen würde. Sie fanden einen schönen Topf, legten den **Dünger** ein, einen Thermometer, haben ein paar Bücher über Pflanzenanbau gelesen und fuhren mit ihrem Leben fort. Jeden Tag gingen sie zu dem **Topf** und warteten gespannt darauf, dass etwas auftaucht.

Jim was also at this meeting, and as everyone else present, he got the seed, too. When he arrived home, he shared the message with his wife and they decided to nurture the seed from which the plant would grow. They found a nice pot, put the fertilizer, took a thermometer, read a few books on plant cultivation, and continued with their lives. Every day they went to the pot and eagerly waited for something to emerge.

Nach 20 Tagen haben einige von Jims Kollegen bereits angefangen, über ihre wachsenden Pflanzen zu sprechen. Und Jim beobachtete jeden Tag mit seiner Frau, aber nichts passierte. Es ist über ein

Monat vergangen und nichts ist passiert. Über die Pflanzen wurde schon viel diskutiert.

After 20 days, some of Jim's colleagues had already started talking about their growing plants. And Jim watched with his wife every day, but nothing happened. It had been over a month and nothing happened. There had already been a lot of discussion about the plants.

Zur Mittagszeit tauschten sie praktische Ideen über schnellen **Wachstum** aus, und Jim erkannte, dass er als einziger keinen Erfolg hatte.

At lunch-time, they exchanged practical ideas of rapid growth, and Jim realized that he was alone with nothing and that he was unsuccessful.

Sechs Monate später, und es gab immer noch keine Fortschritte. Er begann zu glauben, dass er einen Fehler gemacht hatte. Vielleicht zu viel Wasser oder schlechter Dünger oder etwas anderes, das er nicht erklären konnte. Er wusste, dass er sein Bestes gab und es tat ihm leid, dass er keine Ergebnisse hatte.

Six months later, and there was still no progress. He began to believe that he had made a mistake. Maybe too much water or bad fertilizer or something else that he could not explain. He knew he did the best he could and was sorry he had no results.

Das Jahr ging bald zu Ende, und die jungen Bosse versammelten sich mit ihren Pflanzen, um den Geschäftsführer zu treffen. Jim sagte seiner Frau, dass er den leeren Topf nicht nehmen würde, aber sie schaffte es, ihn zu überreden, um den Manager zu erzählen, was passiert war. Er war sehr nervös.

The year soon came to an end, and the young bosses gathered together with their plants to meet the general manager. Jim told his wife that he would not take the empty pot, but she, however, managed to persuade him, telling him to tell the manager fairly what had happened. He was very nervous.

Er dachte, dass dies der unangenehmste Moment für ihn im Leben sein wird. Trotzdem wusste sie, dass sie Recht hatte und war fest davon überzeugt, dass er nichts falsch gemacht hatte. Er nahm seinen Topf in den Besprechungsraum. Er sah wunderschöne Pflanzen auf dem Tisch. Sie waren alle groß und ausgewachsen.

He thought that this would be the most unpleasant moment for him in life. Still, she knew she was right and was firmly convinced that there was nothing he did wrong. He took his pot in the meeting room. He saw beautiful plants on the table. They were all big and fully grown.

Er stellte seinen leeren Topf auf den Boden, während andere lachten. Als der Geschäftsführer ankam, schaute er durch alle Pflanzen und begrüßte die Kandidaten. Jim versuchte, so weit von ihm entfernt zu sein, damit er es nicht sehen würde.

He put his empty pot on the floor, while others were laughing. When the general manager arrived, he looked through all the plants and greeted the candidates. Jim tried to be as far away from him, so that he would not see it.

"Wie schön!" sagte der Geschäftsführer. "Ich sehe, dass es jetzt nicht einfach sein wird, einen neuen Manager auszuwählen ..." Und in diesem Moment sah er den leeren Topf. Er hat den Vizepräsidenten gebeten, es zu nehmen und den **Eigentümer** zu ihm zu bringen. Jim trat heraus.

"How beautiful!" the general manager said. "I see that it will not be easy to pick a new manager now ..." And, at that moment, he saw the empty pot. He asked the vice president take it and bring the owner to him. Jim stepped out.

"Oh Gott ... Vielleicht werde ich jetzt rausgeschmissen", dachte er.

"Oh God ... Maybe I'll get kicked out of the company now," he thought.

Als er kam, fragte ihn der Manager, was mit seinem Samen passierte. Und Jim war ganz ehrlich und er entschuldigte sich. Der Manager bat dann alle zu sitzen - außer Jim. Er sah sie an und sagte:

When he came, the general manager asked him what happened to his seed. And Jim was all honest and he apologized. The general manager then asked everyone to sit - except for Jim. He looked at them and said:

"Jim, ich bin sehr stolz auf dich ... Jim ist der neue CEO der Firma!"

"Jim, I'm very proud of you. Jim is the new CEO of the company!"

"Nun ... wie ist das möglich? Mein Topf ist leer ...", fragte Jim verwirrt.

"Well ... how is that possible? My pot is empty. " Jim asked confused.

Der alte Manager erklärte: "Vor einem Jahr gab ich jedem von euch einen toten Samen. Es war unmöglich, dass etwas daraus wächst. Jeder von euch, der sah, dass nichts passierte, beschloss es durch gesunde Samen zu ersetzen. Jeder von euch - Außer Jim. Ihr alle habt mir Pflanzen und Blumen gebracht. Nur Jim war stolz auf das **Versagen** und hatte genug **Mut** und Ehrlichkeit, mir einen leeren Topf zu bringen. Ihr wolltet Erfolg - um jeden Preis, und Jims Ehrlichkeit war wichtiger als Erfolg. Deshalb ist er heute der CEO ... "

The old general manager explained: "One year ago I gave each of you a dead seed. It was impossible that something could grow out of it. Each of you, seeing nothing to grow, decided to replace it with healthy seeds. Each of you - except Jim. You all brought me plants and flowers. Only Jim was proud of the failure and had enough courage and honesty to bring me an empty seed. You all wanted success - at all cost, and Jim's honesty was more important than success. That is why he is the CEO today. "

Zusammenfassung

Der Manager einer Firma wollte in Rente gehen und musste deswegen einen neuen Manager auswählen. Er gab den Mitarbeitern einen Samen und sagte ihnen, dass sie sich darum kümmern sollen und nach einem Jahr damit zurückkommen sollen, damit der Manager sieht, was sie mit dem Samen gemacht haben. So wird er den neuen Manager auswählen. Einer der Mitarbeiter, Jim, hatte keinen Erfolg mit dem Samen und nach einem Jahr kam er wieder zurück mit seinem leerem Topf. Alle anderen hatten schöne Pflanzen außer Jim. Nachdem der alte Manager sich die Pflanzen ansah, war er fasziniert. Doch dann sah er Jim's Topf. Er sagte, dass Jim der neue Manager ist. Alle waren geschockt und Jim fragte warum er den Job bekommen hat. Der Manager erklärte, dass er vor einem Jahr jedem von ihnen einen toten Samen gegeben hat. Jeder von den Mitarbeitern hat den Samen durch einen gesunden ersetzt, außer Jim. Deswegen hat Jim gewonnen, weil er ehrlich war und den Manager nicht angelogen hat.

Summary

The manager of a company wanted to retire and therefore had to select a new manager. He gave the staff a seed and told them to take care of it, and after a year they had to come back with it so the manager could see what they had done with the seed. This is how he would pick the new manager. One of the co-workers, Jim, was unsuccessful with the seed and after a year he came back with his empty pot. Everyone else had nice plants except Jim. After the old manager looked at the plants, he was fascinated. But then he saw Jim's pot. He decided that Jim was the new manager. Everyone was shocked and Jim asked why he got the job. The manager explained that a year ago he gave each of them a dead seed. Every worker replaced the seed with a healthy one except for Jim. That's why Jim won, because he was honest and did not lie to the manager.

Wortschatz(Vocabulary)

Geschäftsmann – business man

Ruhestand - retirement

Geschäftsführer - manager

Samen - seed

Gießt (gießen) – to water

Treffen - meeting

Pflanze - plant

Dünger - fertilizer

Topf - pot

Wachstum - growth

Eigentümer - owner

Versagen - failure

Mut – courage

Fragen

1. Warum musste der Geschäftsführer einen neuen Manager auswählen?

2. Wie heißt der Mitarbeiter mit dem leeren Topf?

3. Was gab der Geschäftsführer den Mitarbeitern?

4. Wie lange mussten sich die Mitarbeiter um den Samen kümmern?

5. Wer hat Jim geholfen?

6. Wo hat Jim den Samen aufbewahrt?

a. in dem Kühlschrank

b. unter dem Kissen

c. in einem Topf

7. Warum war Jim nervös?

a. weil er den Samen verloren hat

b. weil jemand den Samen geklaut hat

c. weil der Samen nicht gewachsen hat

8. Wie sahen die Samen von den anderen nach einem Jahr aus?

a. jeder hat einen leeren Topf mitgebracht

b. jeder andere hatte eine schöne Pflanze

c. die Samen waren tot

9. Wer wurde der neue Geschäftsführer?

a. Jim

b. Jim's Frau

c. ein anderer Mitarbeiter

10. Warum war Jims Topf leer?

a. weil der Samen tot war

b. weil Jim den Samen verloren hat

c. weil er sich nicht um den Samen gut gekümmert hat

Questions

1. Why did the manager have to choose a new manager?

2. What is the name of the employee with the empty pot?

3. What did the manager give the employees?

4. How long did the staff have to take care of the seed?

5. Who helped Jim?

6. Where did Jim save the seed?

a. in the fridge

b. under the pillow

c. in a pot

7. Why was Jim nervous?

a. because he lost the seed

b. because someone has stolen the seed

c. because the seed did not grow

8. What did the seeds look like after another year?

a. Everyone brought an empty pot

b. Everyone else had a beautiful plant

c. the seeds were dead

9. Who became the new managing director?

a. Jim

b. Jim's wife

c. other employee

10. Why was Jim's pot empty?

a. because the seed was dead

b. because Jim lost the seed

c. because he did not take good care of the seed

Antworten

1. Weil er in Rente gehen wollte.

2. Jim

3. Einen Samen

4. Ein Jahr lang.

5. Seine Frau

6. c

7. c

8. c

9. b

10.a

Answers

1. Because he wanted to retire.

2. Jim

3. One seed

4. One year

5. His wife

6. c

7. c

8. c

9. b

10. a

Chapter 4 – Ein wahrer Freund (A true friend)

Da war mal ein Junge namens Kevin. Er hatte viele Freunde. Aber was es bedeutet, einen richtigen Freund zu haben, hat er an einem sonnigen Tag gelernt, als er und seine Freunde beschlossen, nach der Schule Fußball zu spielen.

There was a boy named Kevin. He had a lot of friends. But he learned what it means to have a friend one sunny day when he and his friends decided to play football after school.

Sie alle versammelten sich auf dem **Spielplatz** hinter der Schule. Dort waren seine besten Freunde: Leo, Paul, Mark, Marcus, Tim, Ricky und Willie. Also haben sie sich in zwei Teams aufgeteilt. Kevin landete mit Leo, Paul und Willie in einem Team. Die Sonne schien so stark, dass sie in einem Moment sich kaum sehen konnten.

They all gathered on the playground behind the school. There were all his best friends there: Leo, Paul, Mark, Marcus, Tim, Ricky and Willie. So they divided into two teams. Kevin ended up in the team with Leo, Paul and Willie. The sun was shining so hard that at one point they began to squint and they could hardly see each other.

Und gerade als er sich auf den perfekten **Schuss** vorbereitete, blendete die Sonne ihn mit seinem **überwältigenden** Glanz. Kevin verfehlte den Ball und er spürte, dass der Boden unter seinen Füßen fiel. Er keuchte in der Luft und fiel mit einem lauten Krachen zu **Boden**. "Dumm, wie konntest du es nicht treffen?" Kevin hörte Willie's **Stimme**, als er versuchte vom Boden aufzustehen. Alles tat weh.

And just when he was preparing to make the perfect hit, the sun blinded him with its overwhelming shine. Kevin missed the ball, and he felt as though the ground was falling under his feet. He gasped in the air and with a loud crash fell to the floor. "Dumb, how did you miss it!" Kevin heard Willie's voice as he tried to get up from the floor. Everything hurt.

"Meine **Großmutter** hätte es besser machen können!" Ricky **kicherte**. "Die Sonne hat mich **erschüttert**!" Kevin verteidigte sich. "Ja sicher!" Leo lachte auch. Kevin befand sich mitten in den **Vorwürfen** des Schmerzes in seinem ganzen Körper, und er fühlte die **Schmerzen** am meisten in seinem Herzen. Er fühlte sich verletzt, weil seine Freunde ihn ausgelacht haben.

"My grandmother would have kicked it right!" Ricky giggled. "The sun shook me!" Kevin defended. "Yeah, sure!" Leo laughed as well. Kevin found himself in the midst of the accusations as pain was in his whole body, and he felt the most in his heart. He was tired of it because his friends were ridiculing him.

Er schaffte es, aufzustehen und mit großen Schmerzen auf die Füße zu kommen. Er sah das rote, leuchtende **Blut** über sein **Knie** fließen. In der **Ferne** sah er Willie und Ricky wie sie seinen Sturz nachahmen und die anderen lachten über die **Vorstellung.**

He managed to stand up to his feet with great pain. He saw the red, shining blood flowing down his knee. In the distance he saw Willie and Ricky imitate his fall and the others laughed at the performance.

Dann kam Marcus besorgt zu ihm und sah ihn an: "Geht es dir gut?" fragte er. Kevin rieb sich leicht den Kopf. "Du weißt, ich glaube nicht, dass sie Recht haben und ich denke, es war ein guter **Versuch.**

Du solltest dich nicht von den Meinungen derer stören lassen, die nicht wirklich deine Freunde sind", sagte Marcus leise und half Kevin, sich auf die Bank neben dem Spielplatz zu setzen.

Then Marcus came to him worriedly, looking at him, "Are you okay?" he asked. Kevin rubbed his head slightly. "You know I do not think they're right and I actually think it was a good try. You should not be bothered by the opinions of those who are not really your friends, " Marcus said quietly, helping Kevin to sit on the bench next to the playground.

Dann rief er den anderen Jungs zu, dass sie sich in dieser Halbzeit ausruhen würden. Dann setzte er sich und sagte zu Kevin: "Weißt du, mit solchen Freunden musst du vorsichtig sein. Ich sage nicht, dass du nicht mit ihnen rumhängen sollst, aber du musst den Unterschied zwischen Freunden und echten Freunden kennen. Sonst wirst du dich verletzen!

Then he shouted to the other boys that they would rest this half-time. Then he sat down and said to Kevin: "You know with such friends you need to be careful. I do not say you do not have to hang out with them, but you have to know the difference between friends and real friends. Otherwise it can hurt you! "

Zusammenfassung

Kevin spielte Fußball an einem sonnigen Tag mit seinen besten Freunden. Als Kevin einen Schuss machen wollte, hat ihn die Sonne geblendet und er hat den Ball verpasst. Er fiel auf den Boden und hat das Knie verletzt. Alle haben ihn ausgelacht außer Marcus. Kevin fühlte sich schlecht und verletzt. Marcus hat ihn geholfen und mit ihm gesprochen. Er hat zu Kevin gesagt, dass er wissen muss, wer seine wahren Freunde sind, denn ansonsten wird er sich wieder verletzen.

Summary

Kevin played football on a sunny day with his best friends. When Kevin wanted to take a shot, the sun blinded him and he missed the ball. He fell to the ground and injured his knee. Everyone laughed at him except Marcus. Kevin felt bad and hurt. Marcus helped him and talked to him. He told Kevin that he needed to know who his true friends were, otherwise he'd hurt himself again.

Wortschatz (Vocabulary)

Spielplatz - playground

Schuss - kick

überwältigenden - overwhelming

Boden - ground

Stimme - voice

Großmutter - grandmother

erschüttert - shocked

Vorwürfen - accusations

Schmerzen - pain

Blut - blood

Knie - knee

Ferne - distance

Vorstellung - performance

Versuch – try

kicherte - giggled

Questions

1. Was haben die Jungs gespielt?

2. Wann haben sie gespielt?

3. Wie heißt der Junge der sich verletzt hat?

4. Was passiert mit Kevin?

5. Wer lacht ihn aus?

6. Wer hat gekichert?

a. Willie

b. Marcus

c. Ricky

7. Wer hat Kevin geholfen?

a. Marcus

b. Paul

c. Willie

8. Warum hat Kevin den Ball nicht getroffen?

a. wegen dem Schnee

b. weil ihn die Sonne geblendet hat

c. wegen dem Regen

9. Was tut Kevin weh?

a. der Arm

b. der Finger

c. das Knie

10. Was sagt Marcus zu Kevin?

a. dass er dumm ist

b. dass er blutet

c. dass er wissen muss wer seine wahren Freunde sind

Questions

1. What did the boys play?

2. When did they play?

3. What's the name of the boy who got hurt?

4. What happens to Kevin?

5. Who is laughing at him?

6. Who giggled?

a. Willie

b. Marcus

c. Ricky

7. Who helped Kevin?

a. Marcus

b. Paul

c. Willie

8. Why did not Kevin hit the ball?

a. because of the snow

b. because the sun blinded him

c. because of the rain

9. Where does Kevin feel pain?

a. the arm

b. the finger

c. the knee

10. What does Marcus say to Kevin?

a. that he is stupid

b. that he is bleeding

c. that he needs to know who his true friends are

Antworten

1. Fußball

2. Nach der Schule

3. Kevin

4. Er trifft den Ball nicht und er verletzt sich

5. Seine Freunde

6. c

7. a

8. b

9. c

10. c

Answers

1. Football

2. After school

3. Kevin

4. He does not hit the ball and he gets hurt

5. His friends

6. c

7. a

8. b

9. c

10. c

Chapter 5 – Schalen aus Holz (Wooden bowls)

Ein träger alter Mann lebte mit seinem Sohn, seiner **Schwiegertochter** und seinem vierjährigen **Enkel**. Die Hände des alten Mannes **zitterten**, seine Sicht war schwach und seine Beine dienten ihm nicht sehr gut.

A sluggish old man lived with his son, daughter in law, and four-year-old grandson. The old man's hands shivered, his vision was weak, and his legs did not serve him very well.

Als die Familie sich zum Essen an den Tisch setzen würde, würden die zitternden Hände des Großvaters und die geringe **Sehkraft** das Essen sehr schwierig und unangenehm machen. Das Essen würde vom **Löffel** auf den Boden fallen. Wenn er das Glas heben wollte, würde die Milch auf den Tisch fallen. Sein Sohn und seine Schwiegertochter begannen wütend zu werden. "Wir müssen etwas mit unserem Großvater machen", sagte der Sohn eines Tages. Ich habe genug von der verschütteten Milch, lautem Essen und Essen auf dem Boden. Der Sohn und die Schwiegertochter stellten einen kleinen Tisch in die **Ecke** des Zimmers auf.

When the family would sit down at the table to eat, the grandfather's shaking hands and low vision would make the meal very difficult and unpleasant. The food would fall from the spoon to the floor. If he wanted to get a glass, the milk would go down on the table. His son and daughter in law started to get angry. "We have to do something with our grandfather," said the son one day. I have enough of the spilled milk, loud eating and food on the floor." The son and daughter in law set up a small table in the corner of the room.

Der Großvater aß dort, während der Rest der Familie das Essen genoss. Als der Großvater ein paar **Schalen** zerbrach, wurde sein Essen in einer Holzschale serviert. Wenn die Familie manchmal den Großvater ansah, sahen sie manchmal die Tränen in seinen Augen, als er allein da saß. Dennoch, die einzigen Worte, die das junge Paar für ihn hatte, waren Worte der **Wut**, wenn etwas auf den Boden fiel.

The grandfather was eating there, while the rest of the family enjoyed the meal. After the grandfather had broken a few bowls, his food was served in a wooden bowl. When the family looked at the grandfather, they would sometimes see the tears in his eyes as he sat there alone. Nevertheless, the only words the young couple had for him were words of anger if something fell to the floor.

Der vierjährige Enkel sah **schweigend** zu. Eines Abends vor dem Essen sah sein Vater seinen kleinen Sohn mit Holzstücken spielen. Er fragte ihn: "Was machst du?" Der Junge antwortete: "Oh, ich mache kleine Schalen aus **Holz** für dich und Mutter, damit ihr etwas habt, woraus ihr essen könnt, wenn ich groß bin." Der Junge lächelte und fuhr mit seiner Arbeit fort.

The four-year-old grandson looked in silence. One evening before a meal, his father saw his little son playing with pieces of wood. He asked him, "What are you doing?" The boy replied, "Oh, I'm making small wooden pans for you and mom to have something to eat from when I grow up." The boy smiled and continued with his job.

Die Eltern waren sprachlos, und **Tränen** liefen über ihre **Wangen**. Obwohl sie kein Wort sagten, wussten beide, was jetzt zu tun war. An diesem Abend nahmen sie den alten Mann an der Hand und brachten ihn sanft zu seinem Tisch. Bis zum Ende seines Lebens aß der alte Mann mit seiner Familie. Interessanterweise waren weder Sohn noch Tochter besorgt, wenn Milch verschüttet wurde oder wenn das Essen auf den Boden fiel.

The parents were left speechless and their tears began to run down their cheeks. Although they did not speak a word, they both knew what to do. That evening they took the old man by the hand and gently brought him to his table. By the end of his life, the old man ate with his family. Interestingly, neither son nor daughter were worried when milk was spilled or when the food fell on the floor.

Zusammenfassung

Ein alter Mann lebte mit seinem Sohn, Schwiegertochter und Enkel zusammen. Da der Mann sehr alt war, konnte er nicht leicht essen und trinken und oft fiel ihm das Essen auf den Boden oder er würde Milch verschütten. Dies ärgerte seinen Sohn und Schwiegertochter und deswegen stellten sie einen Tisch in der Ecke für ihn auf. Dort aß er aus Schalen aus Holz, weil er die anderen gebrochen hat. Eines Abends spielte der Enkel mit Holz und der Vater fragte ihn was er macht. Sein Sohn sagt ihm, dass er Schalen aus Holz macht, damit er und seine Mutter diese zum Essen benutzen können, wenn er groß wird. Seine Eltern haben danach verstanden, dass sie den Großvater schlecht behandelt haben und brachten ihn wieder zum Tisch damit er mit seiner Familie zusammen essen kann. Sie haben sich nie wieder über ihn beklagt.

Summary

An old man lived with his son, daughter-in-law and grandson. As the man was very old, he could not easily eat and drink and often the food fell to the ground or he would spill his milk. This annoyed his son and daughter-in-law, so they set up a table in the corner for him. There he ate from wooden bowls because he broke the others. One night the grandson played with wood and the father asked him what he was doing. His son told him that he makes wooden bowls so that he and his mother can use them to eat when he grows up. His parents then understood that they had treated the grandfather badly and brought him back to the table so he could eat together with his family. They never complained about him again.

Wortschatz (Vocabulary)

Schwiegertochter – daughter-in-law

Enkel - grandson

Zitterten - shaking

Sehkraft - sight

Löffel - spoon

Ecke - corner

Schalen - bowls

Wut - anger

Schweigend - silently

Holz - wood

Tränen - tears

Wangen – cheeks

Fragen

1. Mit wem lebte der alte Mann?

2. Was fiel dem Mann auf den Boden?

3. Wer war wütend auf den alten Mann?

4. Was haben die Eltern in der Ecke aufgestellt?

5. Warum haben sie dies gemacht?

6. Woraus aß der Großvater?

a. aus einem Teller

b. aus einer Schale aus Holz

c. aus einem Glas

7.Was sah die Familie in den Augen des alten Mannes?

a.Tränen

b.Wut

c.Liebe

8.Was hat der Mann verschüttet?

a.Saft

b.Wasser

c.Milch

9.Wer hat mit Holz gespielt und eine Schale gemacht?

a.der Enkel

b.die Schwiegertochter

c.der Großvater

10. Was haben die Eltern am Ende gemacht?

a.sie brachten den Großvater wieder zum Tisch

b.sie haben den Großvater aus dem Haus gebracht

c.sie haben Schalen aus Holz gemacht

Questions

1.Who did the old man live with?

2.What fell on the ground?

3.Who was mad at the old man?

4.What did the parents set up in the corner?

5. Why have they done this?

6.From what did the grandfather eat?

a. from a plate

b. from a wooden bowl

c. from a glass

7. What did the family see in the eyes of the old man?

a. Tears

b. Anger

c. Love

8. What did the man spill?

a. Juice

b. Water

c. Milk

9. Who played with wood and made a bowl?

a. the grandson

b. the daughter-in-law

c. the grandfather

10. What did the parents do in the end?

a. They brought the grandfather back to the table

b. They brought the grandfather out of the house

c. They made wooden bowls

Antworten

1. Mit seinem Sohn, Schwiegertochter und Enkel

2. Essen

3. Sein Sohn und Schwiegertochter

4. Einen Tisch für den alten Mann

5. Damit er sie nicht beim Essen stört

6. b

7. a

8.c

9.a

10. a

Answers

1.With his son, daughter-in-law and grandson

2.Food

3. His son and daughter-in-law

4.A table for the old man

5.So that he would not bother them while eating

6.b

7.a

8.c

9.a

10. a

Chapter 6 – Eine Brücke des Friedens (A peaceful bridge)

Es gab einmal zwei Brüder, die auf benachbarten Farmen lebten. Eiens Tagesbegannen sie einen ernsthaften **Streit**. Es war der erste große Streit seit vierzig Jahren, als sie Seite an Seite lebten, **Werkzeuge** teilten und sich gegenseitig hielfen.

There were once two brothers who lived on neighbouring farms and they were starting a serious fight. It was the first big fight for forty years, as they lived side by side, sharing tools and helping each other.

Und dann war die Bindung gebrochen. Alles begann mit einem kleinen **Missverständnis,** das zu einem großen Streit und unhöflichen Worten führte, gefolgt von Wochen im **Schweigen.**

And then the bond was broken. It all started with a little misunderstanding that led to a big quarrel and rude words, followed by weeks in silence.

Eines Morgens **klopfte** jemand an Johns Tür. Er öffnete sie und sah einen Mann mit einem Werkzeugkasten. "Ich suche Arbeit", sagte er. "Vielleicht kann ich hier auf deiner Farm Arbeit finden?"

One morning, someone knocked on John's door. He opened it and saw a man with a tool-box. "I'm looking for a job," he said. "Maybe here on your farm I can find some work?"

"Ja", sagte der ältere Bruder. "Ich weiß, was du für mich tun könntest. Siehst du das Haus auf der anderen Seite des Baches? Hier wohnt mein Nachbar; eigentlich ist er mein jüngerer Bruder. Letzte Woche war eine **Wiese** zwischen uns, aber er hat etwas von dem Fluss gegraben und jetzt, ist ein **Bach** zwischen uns. Er hat es gemacht, um mich wütend zu machen, aber ich werde mich jetzt rechen ... Du siehst diesen **Stamm** neben der **Scheune**? Ich will, dass du einen zwei Meter langen **Zaun** baust, damit ich ihn und sein Haus nicht mehr sehen kann. "

"Yes," said the older brother. "I know what you could do for me. You see that house on the other side of the stream? This is where my neighbour lives - actually, my younger brother. Last week, there was a meadow between us, but he dug something from the river to here and now there is a stream between us. He did it to make me angry, but I'll get back at him ... You see that trunk by the barn? I want you to make me a two-meter-long fence so I cannot even see him or his house anymore. "

Der Mann sagte: "Ich verstehe alles. Geben Sie mir **Nagel** und **Bohrer** und ich werde eien tolle Arbeit machen."

The man said, "I understand everything. Give me a nail and a drill and I will do a great job. "

Der ältere Bruder musste in die Stadt gehen, also gab er dem Mann das nötige Material und ging weg. Der Mann arbeitete den ganzen Tag.

The older brother had to go to the city, so he gave the carpenter the necessary material and left. The man worked all day.

Als der ältere Bruder um **Mitternacht** zurückkehrte, beendete der Mann die Arbeit. Er war geschockt! Es gab überhaupt keinen Zaun. Er baute eine **Brücke**, die die beiden **Ufer** des Baches verband. Es war eine schöne Brücke, und von seiner anderen Seite näherte sich sein jüngerer Bruder.

As the elder brother returned at midnight, the carpenter finished the job. He was shocked! There was no fence at all. He made a bridge that connected the two banks of the stream. It was a beautiful bridge, and from his other side, his younger brother approached him.

"Du bist wirklich ein großartiger Mann, da du nach allem, was ich getan habe, die Brücke gebaut hast", sagte der jüngere Bruder.

"You're really a great man when you made the bridge after everything I have done," said the younger brother.

Die Brüder standen jeweils auf ihrer Seite der Brücke, und so machten sie sich langsam auf den Weg und trafen sich in der Mitte. Sie sahen, dass der Man seinen **Werkzeugkasten** aufhob und gehen wollte. "Hey, warte! Bleib ein paar Tage bei uns, es gibt noch viele Dinge, die du tun kannst", sagte der ältere Bruder.

Brothers stood each on their side of the bridge, so they slowly set out to meet each other, settling in the middle. They saw that the worker raised his toolbox and wanted to leave. "Hey, wait! Stay with us for a few days. There are many more things you can do," said the older brother.

"Ich würde es gerne", sagte der Mann, "aber ich muss noch viele Brücken bauen."

"I would love to," said the carpenter, "but I need to build many more bridges."

Zusammenfassung

Zwei Brüder hatten ihre eigenen Farmen und lebten in Frieden. Eines Tages hatten sie einen Streit und der ältere Bruder entschied sich, einen Mann anzustellen, der einen riesigen Zaun baut, damit er die Farm und das Haus seines jüngeren Bruders nicht mehr sehen kann. Der Mann hat gesagt, dass er den Job macht. Als der ältere Bruder am Ende des Tages nach Hause kam, sah er, dass der Mann keinen Zaun, sondern eine Brücke über dem Fluss gemacht hat, der die beiden Farmen teilte. Die zwei Brüder waren erstaunt und bedankten sich bei dem Mann. Danach fragten sie ihn, ob er noch bleiben könnte und weiter für sie arbeitet, doch der Mann sagte, dass er leider gehen muss, da er noch viele andere Brücken bauen muss.

Summary

Two brothers had their own farms and lived in peace. One day they had a fight and the older brother decided to hire a man to build a huge fence so he would not be able to see his younger brother's farm and house. The man said that he would do the work. When the elder brother returned home at the end of the day, he saw that the man had not made a fence, but a bridge over the river that divided the two farms. The two brothers were shocked and thanked the man. Then they asked him if he could stay and continue to work for them, but the man said that unfortunately he had to leave as he had to build many other bridges.

Wortschatz (Vocabulary)

Streit – conflict/argument

Werkzeuge - tools

Missverständnis - misunderstanding

Schweigen - silence

Klopfte - knocked

Wiese - meadow

Bach - stream

Stamm - stem

Scheune - barn

Zaun - fence

Nagel - spike

Bohrer - drill

Mitternacht - midnight

Brücke - bridge

Ufer - shore

Werkzeugkasten – tool-box

Fragen

1. Was hatten die beiden Brüder?

2. Welcher Bruder hat einen Arbeiter eingestellt?

3. Was musste der Arbeiter bauen?

4. Wo ging der ältere Bruder nachdem er mit dem Arbeiter gesprochen hat?

5. Was hat der Arbeiter mitgebracht?

6. Was stand zwischen den Farmen der beiden Brüder?

a. ein Wald

b. ein Fluss

c. ein Spielplatz

7. Was hat der Arbeiter am Ende gebaut?

a. eine Brücke

b. ein Gebäude

c. eine Bank

8. Wie begann der ganze Streit zwischen den Brüdern?

a. sie haben sich jahrelang gestritten

b. mit einem kleinem Missverständnis

c. der jüngere Bruder hat etwas geklaut

9. Was wollte der ältere Bruder bauen?

a. eine Brücke

b. einen Tisch

c. einen Zaun

10. Was hat der Arbeiter am Ende gesagt?

a. dass er noch viele Brücken bauen muss

b. dass er gerne zum Abendessen bleiben wird

c. dass er weiter für die Brüder arbeiten wird

Questions

1. What did the two brothers have?

2. Which brother hired a worker?

3. What did the worker have to build?

4. Where did the older brother go after talking to the worker?

5. What did the worker bring?

6. What stood between the farms of the two brothers?

a. a forest

b. a river

c. a playground

7. What did the worker build in the end?

a. a bridge

b. a building

c. a bank

8. How did the whole fight between the brothers begin?

a. They argued for years

b. with a little misunderstanding

c. the younger brother stole something

9. What did the older brother want to build?

a. a bridge

b. a table

c. a fence

10. What did the worker say in the end?

a. that he still has to build many bridges

b. that he would like to stay for dinner

c. that he will continue to work for the brothers

Antworten

1. Farmen

2. Der ältere Bruder

3. Einen Zaun

4. Er ging in die Stadt

5. Einen Werkzeugkasten

6. b

7. a

8. b

9. c

10. a

Answers

1. Farms

2. The older brother

3. A fence

4. He went to the city

5. A toolbox

6. b

7. a
8. b
9. c
10. a

Chapter 7 – Du bist was du denkst (You are what you think)

Zu Beginn des Schuljahres rief der Direktor einer **Grundschule** drei Lehrer an, und teilte ihnen mit, dass sie im letzten Schuljahr die besten Lehrer waren. Er sagte ihnen dann, dass sie im nächsten **Schuljahr** drei **Abteilungen** unterrichten sollten, die aus 90 der intelligentesten Schülern bestehen. Aber er sagte ihnen, dass es eine **Bedingung** gäbe, und diese ist, dass sie ihren Schülern nichts sagen dürfen, damit sie ihre Eltern oder die Eltern von Kindern aus anderen Abteilungen nicht stören.

At the beginning of the school year, the director of one primary school called three teachers and informed them that they were the best teachers in the last school year. He then told them that in the next school year they should teach three departments that consist of 90 of the most intelligent students. But they told them that there was one condition, and that was to say nothing to their students, so they would not disturb their parents or the parents of children from other departments.

Das Schuljahr begann und kamm zu einem Ende. Am Ende des Jahres war die **Durchschnittsnote** für Schüler dieser drei Klassen viel besser als für andere Klassen in ihrer Schule, und sogar 20 bis

30% ihres Erfolges waren besser als der Durchschnitt aller Schulen in der Gegend.

The school year started and finished. At the end of the year, the average grade for students from these three classes was much better than other classes in their school, and even 20 to 30% of their success was better than the average of all schools in the area.

Als der Direktor die Lehrer fragte, was sie darüber dachten, wie sie es geschafft hatten, sagten sie ihm, dass dies eine wundervolle **Erfahrung** für sie sei, dass ihre Arbeit jedoch dadurch erleichtert wurde, dass sie begabte und erfolgreiche Schüler unterrichteten.

When the director asked the teachers what they thought about it and how they achieved it, they told him that this had been a wonderful experience for them, but that their work was made easier by the fact that they taught gifted and successful students.

Der Direktor sagte zu ihnen: "Lassen Sie mich Ihnen die wahre **Wahrheit** sagen: Sie waren weder begabt noch besonders intelligente Schüler, wie wir Ihnen am Anfang sagten, sondern wählten zufällig 90 Schüler aus, die wir in diesen drei Abteilungen eingesetzt haben.

The director told them: "Let me tell you the true truth: Those were not gifted, nor especially intelligent students, as we told you at the beginning, but a randomly selected 90 students that we deployed into those three departments that you taught.

Die Lehrer waren **verwirrt:** "Haben wir zum Erfolg des Schülers **beigetragen**?"

The teachers were confused: "Well, did we contribute to the students' success?"

Der Direktor sagte ihnen: "Nun lassen Sie mich Ihnen eine andere Wahrheit sagen - ich wählte sie, indem ich die Namen aller Lehrer in der Schule auf ein **Blatt** Papier schrieb, und dann zeigte ich mit meinem Finger auf drei Namen - das waren eure Namen."

The director told them, "Now let me admit to you another truth - I chose you by writing the names of all teachers in the school on a sheet of paper, and then I pointed my finger at three names - these were your names."

"Also, was ist der **Grund**?" Sie fragten.

"So what's the reason?" They asked.

„Der Grund dafür war es, dass ihr zunächst den **Standpunkt** vertretet habt, dass ihr erfolgreich sein werdet, basierend auf die Information die euch dazu gebracht hat, so zu denken; also habt ihr das Ergebnis erreicht, auch wenn diese Information nicht korrekt war. Ich wollte euch zeigen, dass ihr das Ergebnis dessen seit, was ihr denkt und glaubt."

"The reason is that you initially had the stance that you will achieve success based on the information that led you to expect extraordinary success, so you have achieved the result, regardless of the fact that this information was incorrect. I wanted to show you that you are the result of what you think and what you are hoping for."

Die Lehrer waren beeindruckt und dankbar für die Lektion, die sie gelernt haben.

The teachers were impressed and thankful for the lesson they'd learned.

Zusammenfassung

In einer Grundschule wählte der Direktor drei Lehrer aus und sagte ihnen, dass sie die besten Lehrer seien und dass sie im nächsten Schüljahr die 90 intelligentesten Schüler unterrichten werden. Er hat sie aber gebeten, nichts darüber zu sagen, damit die anderen Schüler und Eltern sich nicht ärgern. Am Ende des Schuljahres hatten diese Klassen die besten Ergebnisse von allen. Die Lehrer meinten, dass es viel einfacher war, da sie begabte Schüler unterrichteten. Doch der Direktor verriet ihnen dann ein Geheimnis, undzwar, dass diese Schüler ganz normale Schüler waren und dass er die Lehrer ausgewählt hat, indem er einfach auf drei Namen mit dem Finger zeigte. Die Lehrer waren verwirrt und fragten warum er dies gemacht hat und der Direktor sagte ihnen, dass er ihnen zeigen wollte, wie ihre eigenen Gedanken ihnen helfen können, erfolgreich zu sein.

Summary

In a primary school, the director selected three teachers and told them that they were the best teachers and that they would teach the 90 most intelligent students in the next year. But he asked them not to say anything so that the other students and parents would not get angry. At the end of the school year, these classes had the best results of all. The teachers thought it was a lot easier as they had taught gifted students. But the director had then revealed a secret to them, that these students were ordinary students and that he had selected the teachers by simply pointing at three names with his finger. The teachers were confused and asked why he had done this, and the director told them that he wanted to show them how their own thoughts can help them succeed.

Wortschatz (Vocabulary)

Grundschule – primary school

Schuljahr – school year

Abteilungen - departments

Bedingung - condition

Durschnittsnote – average grade

Erfahrung - experience

Wahrheit - truth

verwirrt - confused

beigetragen - contributed

Blatt - sheet

Grund - reason

Standpunkt - stance

Fragen

1. Wer hat die Lehrer ausgewählt?
2. Wie viele Lehrer wurden ausgewählt?
3. Wie viele Schüler wurden ausgewählt?
4. Was war die Bedingung?
5. Wie lange mussten die Lehrer diese Schüler unterrichten?
6. In wie viele Abteilungen wurden die Schüler geteilt?
a. zwei
b. fünf
c. drei
7. Wie fühlten sich die Lehrer am Ende des Schuljahres?
a. sie waren erschöpft
b. sie waren wütend
c. sie meinten, dass es sehr leicht war, da es begabte Schüler waren
8. Was hat der Direktor ihnen mitgeteilt?
a. dass es keine begabten Schüler waren
b. dass sie keinen guten Job gemacht haben
c. dass die Schüler schlecht sind
9. Was fragten die Lehrer danach?
a. Was der Grund dafür war
b. Ob die Eltern verärgert sind
c. Welche Schüler die besten Ergebnisse hatten
10. Was wollte der Direktor ihnen zeigen?
a. dass sie schlechte Lehrer sind

b. dass ihre Gedanken den Erfolg beeinflussen

c. dass sie manchmal lügen müssen

Questions

1. Who chose the teachers?

2. How many teachers have been selected?

3. How many students were selected?

4. What was the condition?

5. How long did the teachers have to teach these students?

6. In how many departments were the students divided?

a. two

b. five

c. three

7. How did the teachers feel at the end of the school year?

a. They were exhausted

b. They were angry

c. They thought that it was very easy as those were gifted students

8. What did the director tell them?

a. that they were not gifted students

b. that they did not do a good job

c. that the students are bad

9. What did the teachers ask?

a. what was the reason

b. if the parents were upset

c. which students had the best results

10. What did the director want to show them?

a. that they were bad teachers

b. that their thoughts influence success

c. that sometimes you have to lie

Antworten

1. Der Direktor

2. Drei

3. 90 Schüler

4. dass die Lehrer nichts zu den Schülern oder Eltern sagen

5. Ein Jahr lang

6. c

7. c

8. a

9. a

10. b

Answers

1. The director

2. Three

3. 90 students

4. That the teachers say nothing to the students or parents

5. One year

6. c

7. c

8. a

9. a

10. b

Chapter 8 – Der Taxifahrer (The taxi driver)

Ich habe vor zwanzig Jahren als **Taxifahrer** gearbeitet. Einmal, mitten in der Nacht, kam ich nach einem Anruf zu einem **Gebäude**, das völlig im **Dunkeln** lag, bis auf ein Licht aus dem Fenster im **Erdgeschoss**.

I worked as a taxi driver twenty years ago. Once, in the middle of the night, I arrived at a call in a building that was completely in the dark except for one light from the window on the ground floor.

Unter diesen **Umständen** würden viele Taxifahrer das **Horn** nur ein- oder zweimal benutzen, eine Minute warten und dann losfahren. Aber ich sah zu viele arme Leute, die auf Taxis als einzige **Transportmittel** angewiesen waren. Wenn ich die **Gefahr** in der Luft nicht riechen würde, würde ich immer zur Tür gehen. Ein Passagier könnte jemand sein, der meine Hilfe braucht, dachte ich. Also ging ich zur Tür und klopfte.

Under these circumstances, many taxi drivers would use the horn only once or twice, wait a minute and then drive off. But I saw too many poor people who were dependent on taxis as their only means of transport. If I did not smell the danger in the air, I would always go to the door. A passenger could be someone who needs my help, I thought. So I went to the door and knocked.

"Einen **Augenblick**", sagte eine brüchige, ältere Stimme. Ich hörte etwas auf dem **Boden** ziehen. Die Tür öffnete sich nach einer langen Pause. Vor mir stand eine kleine Frau in ihren Achtzigern. Sie trug ein Kleid mit einem **Muster** und einen Hut, an dem der **Schleier** befestigt war, wie jemand in einem Film aus den 40ern. Neben ihr war ein kleiner Koffer.

"Just a moment," said a brittle, older voice. I heard something pulling on the floor. The door opened after a long pause. In front of me was a small woman in her eighties. She wore a dress with a pattern and a hat on which the veil was attached, like someone from a 40's movie. Next to her was a small suitcase.

Die Wohnung sah aus, als wäre sie jahrelang leer gestanden. Alle **Möbel** waren mit **Laken** bedeckt. Es gab keine Uhren an den **Wänden,** keine kleinen Dinge oder **Geschirr** auf der **Theke.** In der Ecke stand eine **Pappschachtel** voller Fotos und Glaswaren.

The apartment looked like no one had lived in it for years. All the furniture was covered with sheets. There were no clocks on the walls, no small things or dishes on the counter. In the corner was a cardboard box full of photographs and glassware.

"Würden Sie bitte meine Tasche zum Auto bringen" sagte sie. Ich nahm den Koffer zum Taxi, und dann kam ich zurück, um der Frau zu helfen. Sie nahm meine Hand und ging langsam zum Rand des **Bürgersteigs.** Sie dankte mir weiterhin für meine **Freundlichkeit.**

"Would you please take my bag to the car," she said. I took the suitcase to the taxi, and then I came back to help the woman. She took my hand and we walked slowly towards the edge of the sidewalk. She kept on thanking me for my kindness.

"Oh, nichts zu danken", sagte ich ihr. "Ich versuche nur meine Passagiere so zu behandeln, wie ich möchte, dass andere meine Mutter behandeln."

"Oh, no need to thank me," I told her. "I'm just trying to treat my passengers as I would like others to treat my mother."

"Oh, du bist so ein guter Junge", sagte sie. Als wir das Taxi betraten, gab sie mir die Adresse und dann fragte sie mich: "Können wir durch die **Innenstadt** fahren?"

"Oh, you are such a good boy," she said. When we entered the cab, she gave me the address and then she asked me, "Could we go through the city center?"

"Es ist nicht der kürzeste Weg", antwortete ich schnell.

"It's not the shortest way," I replied quickly.

"Das macht nichts", sagte sie. "Ich habe es nicht eilig. Ich bin auf dem Weg ins **Krankenhaus.**"

"It does not matter," she said. "I'm not in a hurry. I'm on my way to the hospital. "

Ich schaute in den Spiegel. Ihre Augen glitzerten.

I looked in the mirror. Her eyes glittered.

"Ich habe keine Familie mehr", fuhr sie fort. "Ärzte sagen, ich habe nicht mehr viel Zeit."

"I no longer have any family," she continued. "Doctors say I don't have a lot of time left."

Ich beugte mich vor und drehte den Taxameter um. "Welchen Weg soll ich nehmen?", Fragte ich.

I leaned in and turned down the taximeter. "Which way would you like to go," I asked.

Wir fuhren für die nächsten zwei Stunden durch die Stadt. Sie zeigte mir das Gebäude, in dem sie als Aufzugsoperator arbeitete. Wir gingen durch die **Nachbarschaft**, wo sie und ihr **Ehemann** lebten. Sie bat mich, vor einem Möbelgeschäft anzuhalten, das früher ein **Tanzsalon** war, in den sie als Mädchen ging. Manchmal hätte sie mich gebeten, vor einem Gebäude oder einer Ecke abzubremsen, und sie saß da und schaute in die Dunkelheit, ohne etwas zu sagen. Als der erste Strahl der Sonne am Horizont erschien, sagte sie plötzlich: "Ich bin müde. Lass uns jetzt gehen."

We drove through the city for the next two hours. She showed me the building where she used to work as an elevator operator. We walked through the neighbourhood where she and her husband lived. She asked me to stop in front of a furniture store that used to be a dancing salon where she was going as a girl. Sometimes she would ask me to slow down in front of some building or corner, and she sat staring into the darkness, not saying anything. When the first rays of the sun began to appear on the horizon, she suddenly said: "I'm tired. Let's go now."

Schweigend fuhren wir zu der Adresse, die sie mir gegeben hatte.

In silence we drove to the address she gave me.

Es war ein kleines Gebäude. Als wir anhielten, kamen zwei Männer zum Taxi. Voller Aufmerksamkeit folgten sie jeder **Bewegung**. Sie müssen sie erwartet haben. Ich öffnete den Kofferraum und nahm den kleinen Koffer zur Tür. Die Frau saß schon im **Rollstuhl.**

It was a small building. Two men came to the taxi as soon as we stopped. Full of attention, they followed every movement. They must have expected her. I opened the trunk and took the small suitcase to the door. The woman was already sitting in wheelchairs.

"Wie viel schulde ich dir?", Fragte sie und öffnete ihre **Handtasche.**

"How much do I owe you," she asked, opening her purse.

"Nichts", antwortete ich.

"Nothing," I replied.

"Du musst von etwas leben", antwortete sie.

"You must live from something," she replied.

"Es gibt andere Passagiere."

"There are other passengers."

Fast ohne nachzudenken, beugte ich mich vor und **umarmte** sie.

Almost without thinking, I leaned over and hugged her.

"Du hast einer alten Frau einen glücklichen Moment geschenkt", sagte sie. "Danke."

"You gave an old woman one moment of happiness," she said. "Thank you."

Ich drückte ihre Hand und ging in das neblige **Morgenlicht.** Hinter mir schloss sich die Tür. Es war der **Klang** des Endes eines Lebens.

I squeezed her hand and walked into the foggy morning light. Behind me, the door closed. It was the sound of the end of life.

In dieser Schicht habe ich keine anderen Passagiere mitgenommen. Ich war in meinen **Gedanken** verloren. Und den Rest des Tages sprach ich kaum. Was wäre, wenn die Frau einen wütenden Fahrer bekommen hätte oder jemanden, der seine **Schicht** beenden wollte? Was, wenn ich mich geweigert hätte, sie mitzunehmen? Wenn ich darüber nachdenke, denke ich, dass es das Wichtigste ist, was ich in meinem Leben getan habe. Wir sind überzeugt, dass sich unser Leben um wichtige Momente dreht. Aber wichtige Momente treffen uns oft **unvorbereitet** - schön verpackt in etwas, das manche als unwichtig bezeichnen würden.

In that shift, I did not take any other passengers. I was lost in my thoughts. And the rest of that day, I barely spoke. What if the woman got an angry driver, or someone who was eager to finish the shift? What if I refused to take her? When I think about it, I think that's the most important thing I've done in my life. We are convinced that we think that our lives revolve around important moments. But important moments often take us unprepared - beautifully packaged in what some would call unimportant.

Zusammenfassung

Ein Taxifahrer erzählt von einer alten Frau, die eines Abends mit ihm durch die Gegend gefahren ist. Sie erzählte ihm, dass sie noch nicht viel Zeit hat und dass sie gerne durch die Stadt fahren möchte, bevor sie ins Krankenhaus geht. Sie haben die ganze Nacht gesprochen und sie hat ihm alle Stellen der Stadt gezeigt, die ihr wichtig waren. Am Ende brachte er sie zum Krankenhaus und verabschiedete sich von ihr. Er wusste, dass er sie nie wieder sehen wird, aber trotzdem war er glücklich, dass er ihre Wünsche erfüllt hat. Er hat gelernt, dass auch solche kleine Gesten für jemanden sehr wichtig sein können.

Summary

A taxi driver tells of an old woman who drove around with him one night. She told him that she did not have much time left and that she would like to drive through the city before she goes to the hospital. They talked the whole night and she showed him all the places in the city that were important to her. In the end he took her to the hospital and said goodbye to her. He knew he would never see her again, but still he was happy that he had fulfilled her wishes. He learned that even such small gestures can be very important for someone else.

Wortschatz (Vocabulary)

Taxifahrer – taxi driver

Gebäude - building

Dunkel – the dark

Erdgeschoss – ground floor

Umständen - circumstances

Horn - horn

Transportmittel - transport

Gefahr - danger

Augenblick - moment

Boden - floor

Muster - pattern

Schleier - veil

Möbel - furniture

Laken - sheet

Wänden - walls

Geschirr - dishes

Theke - counter

Pappschachtel – cardboard box

Bürgersteig - sidewalk

Freundlichkeit - friendliness

Innenstadt – city centre

Krankenhaus - hospital

Nachbarschaft - neighborhood

Ehemann - husband

Tanzsalon – dance studio

Bewegung - movement

Rollstuhl - wheelchair

Handtasche - purse

Umarmte - hugged

Morgenlicht – morning light

Klang - sound

Gedanken - thoughts

Schicht - shift

unvorbereitet - unprepared

Fragen

1. Warum kam der Mann zum Gebäude?

2. Wer hat die Tür geöffnet?

3. Was brach die alte Frau mit sich?

4. Wie sah die Wohnung aus?

5. Auf welchem Geschoss lebte die Frau?

6. Wo musste die Frau hingehen?

a. in ein Restaurant

b. ins Krankenhaus

c. in die Schule

7. Was haben ihr die Ärzte gesagt?

a. dass sie sehr wenig Zeit hat

b. dass sie gesund ist

c. dass sie schwanger ist

8. Der Taxifahrer war:

a. wütend

b. freundlich

c. verärgert

9. Was hat der Taxifahrer am Ende gemacht?

a. er hat Geld für die Fahrt verlangt

b. er hat ihr einen Brief gegeben

c. er hat sie umarmt

10. Was hat er danach gelernt?

a. dass er ein schlechter Mensch ist

b. dass jeder Moment wichtig sein kann

c. dass alte Menschen nett sind

Questions

1. Why did the man come to the building?

2. Who opened the door?

3. What did the old woman carry?

4. What did the apartment look like?

5. On which floor did the woman live?

6. Where did the woman have to go?

a. to a restaurant

b. to the hospital

c .to the school

7. What did the doctors tell her?

a. that she doesn't have much time left

b. that she is healthy

c. that she is pregnant

8. The taxi driver was:

a. angry

b. friendly

c. annoyed

9. What did the taxi driver do in the end?

a. he demanded money for the ride

b. he gave her a letter

c. he hugged her

10. What did he learn after that?

a. that he is a bad person

b. that every moment can be important

c. that old people are nice

Antworten

1. Weil er einen Anruf bekommen hat.

2. Eine alte Frau

3. Einen Koffer

4. Als ob niemand dort lebt.

5. Auf dem Erdgeschoss

6. b

7. a

8. b

9. c

10. b

Answers

1. Because he got a call.

2. An old woman

3. A suitcase

4. As if nobody lives there

5. On the ground floor

6. b

7. a

8. b

9. c

10. b

Chapter 9 – Julia rettet den Kindergarten (Julia saves the kindergarten)

In einer kleinen Stadt lebte eine junge Frau namens Julia Schmidt. Sie war sehr intelligent und talentiert. Da sie Sozialpädagogik studierte, war sie auf der **Suche** nach einem Job in einem Kindergarten. Julia liebte Kinder, und es war schon immer ihr **Traumjob** gewesen. Deswegen beschloss sie, ihre **Bewerbung** in einem kleinen **Kindergarten** abzugeben und dort ihr Glück zu versuchen. Als sie dort ankam, erwartete sie die Direktorin des Kindergartens und **begrüßte** sie.

In a small town lived a young woman named Julia Schmidt. She was very intelligent and talented. Since she was studying social education, she was looking for a job in a kindergarten. Julia loved children and it had always been her dream job. Therefore, she decided to submit her application in a small kindergarten and try her luck there. When she got there, the director of the kindergarten welcomed her.

Julia war nervös, aber sie wollte den Job. Sie stellte sich vor und hat von ihrer Liebe für Kinder erzählt. Außerdem erwähnte sie, dass sie ein **Praktikum** abgeschlossen hat. Die Direktorin hörte Julia zu, aber am Ende sagte sie:

Julia was nervous, but she wanted the job. She introduced herself and told of her love for children. She also mentioned that she had completed an internship. The director listened to Julia, but in the end she said:

„Liebe Frau Schmidt, sie sind sehr freundlich und alles was Sie mir heute erzählt haben ist wundervoll. Ich bin mir sicher, dass Sie eine gute **Erzieherin** sein würden. Ich kann Sie aber nicht **einstellen**. Es tut mir leid."

"Dear Mrs. Schmidt, you are very friendly and all you have told me today is wonderful. I'm sure you would be a good educator. I cannot hire you. I am sorry."

Julia schaute die Frau nervös an.

Julia looked at the woman nervously.

„Können Sie mir bitte sagen, warum Sie dies nicht machen können"?

"Can you please tell me why?"

Die Direktorin antwortete:

The director replied:

„Ich sehe nicht, dass Sie **Erfahrung** in diesem Job haben. Sie können von ihrer Liebe für Kinder reden, aber ich brauche etwas, was mir wirklich sagt, dass Sie für diese Position gut **ausgebildet** sind. Verstehen Sie mich nicht falsch und nehmen sie meine Worte nicht persönlich, aber Sie werden **wahrscheinlich** noch viel arbeiten, bevor Sie als eine kompetente Erzieherin arbeiten können. Ich könnte Sie als **Betreuerin** einstellen. Das bedeutet, dass Sie auf die Kinder während der Schlafenszeit aufpassen. Eine Erzieherin muss wissen, wie man mit Kindern umgeht und was sie tun dürfen und was nicht. Ich habe das **Gefühl,** dass Sie immer noch **unreif** für diese Position sind."

"I do not see that you have experience in this job. You can talk about your love for children, but I need something that really tells me that you are well educated for this position. Do not get me wrong and do not take my words personally, but you probably will work a lot more before you can work as a competent educator. I could hire you as a caregiver. This means that you take care of the children during bedtime. An educator needs to know how to deal with children and what they are allowed to do and what not. I feel like you are still immature for this position. "

Julia sah die Direktorin mit **Enttäuschung** an. Sie fühlte, dass sie mehr als bereit für solch einen Job ist. Für sie war dies ein sehr harter **Schlag** ins Gesicht.

Julia looked at the director with disappointment. She felt that she was more than ready for such a job. For her, this was a very hard slap in the face.

„Frau Schmidt, es tut mir wirklich leid. Sie sind aber sehr jung. Sie haben noch ein ganzes Leben und vielleicht bekommen Sie eines Tages diesen Job. Zurzeit ist dies aber unmöglich für Sie. Ich muss dieses **Gespräch** jetzt zu Ende bringen. Es sind noch andere Kandidaten hier. Viel Glück."

"Mrs. Schmidt, I'm really sorry. But you are very young. You still have a whole life and maybe one day you will get this job. At the moment this is impossible for you. I have to finish this conversation now. There are other candidates here. Good luck."

„Ich verstehe. Danke für Ihre Zeit". Julia hebte ihre Tasche und ging nach draußen. Sie steigte in den Bus und sie konnte ihre Gefühle nicht kontrollieren. Ihre Wangen waren voller Tränen. Sie fühlte sich **gedemütigt** und hatte keine **Hoffnung** mehr. Monate vergingen und sie wusste nicht, wie es weiter gehen soll. Außerdem gab es keine anderen Kindergärten, weil es nicht viele **Bewohner** in der Stadt gab.

"I understand. Thank you for your time." Julia lifted her bag and went outside. She got on the bus and she could not control her feelings. Her cheeks were full of tears. She felt humiliated and had no hope. Months passed and she did not know what to do next. In addition, there were no other kindergartens because there were not many residents in the city.

Eines Morgens ging Julia mit Ihrem Hund in den Park. Sie setzte sich auf eine Bank und nahm die **Zeitungen** aus der Tasche, die sie auf dem Weg gekauft hat. Auf der ersten Seite sah sie ein **Bild** des Kindergartens, in dem sie sich beworben hat. In dem Artikel stand, dass die Direktorin den Kindergarten schließen muss, weil sie nicht genug Geld haben, um alles zu finanzieren. Die Erzieher haben schon seit zwei Monaten kein **Gehalt** bekommen und die Eltern der Kinder sind mit ihrer Arbeit unzufrieden.

One morning Julia went to the park with her dog. She sat down on a bench and took out the newspapers she had bought on the way. On the first page, she saw a picture of the kindergarten she had applied for. The article said that the director had to close the kindergarten because they did not have enough money to finance everything. The educators had not received a salary for two months and the parents of the children were dissatisfied with their work.

Julia war geschockt. Sie wusste, dass sie etwas tun muss. Es handelt sich um Kinder, die Erziehung und Liebe brauchen. Julia ging nach Hause und beschloss, alle Sachen, von ihrem Auto bis zu den paar wertvollen **Kleinigkeiten** zu verkaufen. Das einzige was sie noch übrig hatte, war ihre **Wohnung**, die fast leer war.

Julia was shocked. She knew she had to do something. These were children who needed education and love. Julia went home and decided to sell everything from her car to the few precious little things she had. The only thing she had left was her apartment, which was almost empty.

Danach ging sie in den Kindergarten und **klopfte** auf die Tür der Direktorin.

Then she went to the kindergarten and knocked on the door of the director.

„Guten Tag. Kann ich bitte mit Ihnen sprechen?"

"Good day. Can I speak with you, please? "

Die Direktorin sah erschöpft aus und sah Julia nicht mal an.

The director looked exhausted and did not even look at Julia.

„Sei bitte schnell. Ich habe nicht sehr viel Zeit. Ich muss dieses Büro räumen." – sagte die Direktorin.

"Please be quick. I do not have much time. I have to leave this office," said the director.

„Hier." Julia legte einen großen **Stapel** Geld auf den Tisch.

"Here." Julia put a big stack of money on the table.

Die Direktorin drehte sich zu ihr und sah das Geld.

The director turned to her and saw the money.

„Was ist das?" – fragte sie.

"What's that?" - she asked.

„Ich möchte, dass Sie dieses Geld nehmen und die Kosten decken, die Sie haben. Es kann sicher für einige Monate ausreichen. Ich werde bis dann wieder einen Weg finden und dem Kindergarten helfen" – sagte Julia entschlossen.

"I want you to take this money and cover the costs you have. It can certainly be enough for a few months. I will find a way and help the kindergarten until then," said Julia, determined.

Die Direktorin war geschockt. Ihr kamen sogar die Tränen.

The director was shocked. She even cried.

„Wie habe ich das verdient? Ich habe dich doch vor einigen Monaten abgelehnt und einige Sachen gesagt, die vielleicht zu grob waren."

"How did I deserve that? I refused you a few months ago and said some things that were perhaps too crude. "

„Das ist wahr. Aber mir sind die Kinder wichtig. Manche von ihnen brauchen diesen Kindergarten mehr, als es sie braucht. Deswegen kann ich es nicht zulassen, dass Sie es schließen. Geld sollte kein Problem darstellen. Wenn man Kinder liebevoll behandelt und mit ihnen gut umgeht, dann werden die Eltern auch zufrieden sein und weiterhin ihre Kinder ins Kindergarten schicken. Es ist nicht so kompliziert wie Sie denken."

"This is true. But the children are important to me. Some of them need this kindergarten more than it needs them. That's why I cannot let you close it. Money does not have to be a problem. If you treat children well and with love, then the parents will be satisfied and continue to send their children to kindergarten. It's not as complicated as you think."

Die Direktorin wusste, dass Julia recht hat. Sie sah sie an uns sagte:

The director knew that Julia was right. She looked at her and said:

„Du hast keine Ahnung, wie dankbar ich bin. Das einzige was ich für dich tun kann, ist dich zu bitten, hier mit mir zu arbeiten. Ich kann dir für den Anfang kein großes Gehalt **versprechen**, aber.."

"You have no idea how grateful I am. The only thing I can do for you is to ask you to work here with me. I cannot promise you a big salary for the beginning, but .. "

Julia unterbrach die Direktorin:

Julia interrupted the director:

„Geld ist mir unwichtig. Ich würde gerne hier arbeiten und ich verspreche Ihnen, dass Sie bald wieder aus dieser Situation herauskommen werden."

"Money is unimportant to me. I would like to work here and I promise you that you will get out of this situation soon."

So bekam Julia ihren Traumjob. Ja, die ersten Monate waren hart, aber die Kinder liebten sie. Jeden Tag wuchs die Anzahl der neuen Kinder im Kindergarten und somit auch Julias Liebe für die Kinder.

This is how Julia got her dream job. Yes, the first months were tough, but the kids loved her. The number of new children in the kindergarten grew every day and so did Julia's love for the children.

Zusammenfassung

Julia hatte gerade ihr Studium abgeschlossen und wollte sich für die Position als Erzieherin in dem einzigen Kindergarten in ihrer stadt bewerben. Sie liebte Kinder und wollte den Job sehr. Die Direktorin des Kindergartens gab ihr den Job aber nicht, weil sie meinte Julia hat keine Erfahrung und ist unreif für den Job. Dies war sehr hart für Julia. Eines Tages sah sie aber in der Zeitung, dass die Direktorin den Kindergarten schließen wird, weil es kein Geld mehr gibt und nur wenige Kinder noch da sind. Julia entschloss sich, ihre wertvollen Sachen zu verkaufen und der Direktorin zu helfen. Am Ende war die Direktorin geschockt und hat Julia den Job gegeben. Julia hat den Kindergarten gerettet und jeden Tag kamen neue Kinder, weil sie alle liebten.

Summary

Julia had just completed her studies and wanted to apply for the position of educator in the only kindergarten in her city. She loved children and wanted the job very much. The kindergarten director did not give her the job because she said Julia had no experience and was too immature for the job. This was very hard for Julia. One day, however, she saw in the newspaper that the director had to close the kindergarten because there was no money left and only a few children were still there. Julia decided to sell her precious things and help the director. In the end, the director was shocked and gave Julia the job. Julia saved the kindergarten and every day new children came because they all loved her.

Wortschatz (Vocabulary)

Suche - search

Traumjob – dream job

Bewerbung - application

Kindergarten - kindergarten

begrüßte - greeted

Praktikum - internship

Erzieherin - educator

Einstellen - hire

Erfahrung - experience

ausgebildet - educated

wahrscheinlich - probably

Betreuerin - supervisor

Gefühl - feeling

Unreif - immature

Enttäuschung - dissapointment

Schlag - punch

Gespräch - conversation

gedemütigt - hummiliated

Hoffnung - hope

Bewohner - resident

Zeitungen - newspapers

Bild - photo

Gehalt - salary

Kleinigkeiten – little things

Wohnung - apartment

klopfte - knocked

Stapel - stack

Versprechen – to promise

Fragen

1. Welches Studium hat Julia abgeschlossen?
2. Wo wollte sie sich bewerben?
3. Mit wem hat sie gesprochen?
4. Warum wurde sie abgelehnt?
5. Wo ging Julia mit ihrem Hund?
6. Wie hat Julia die Neuigkeit über den Kindergarten gehört?

a. sie hat er in der Zeitung gelesen

b. ein Freund hat es ihr gesagt

c. die Direktorin hat es ihr mitgeteilt

7. Warum wollte die Direktorin den Kindergarten schließen?

a. weil sie erschöpft war

b. weil sie in eine andere Stadt ziehen musste

c. weil sie es nicht mehr finanzieren konnte

8. Was hat Julia getan?

a. sie hat die Zeitung weggeworfen

b. sie hat ihre wertvollen Sachen verkauft

c. sie hat ihren Hund verkauft

9. Wohin ging Julia mit dem Geld?

a. zum Arzt

b. zu der Direktorin

c. in eine Bank

10. Was passierte am Ende?

a. Julia bekamm den Job als Erzieherin

b. die Direktorin hat sie rausgeschmissen

c. Julia kaufte sich ein neues Auto

Questions

1. What studies did Julia complete?

2. Where did she want to apply?

3. Who did she talk to?

4. Why was she rejected?

5. Where did Julia go with her dog?

6. How did Julia hear the news about the kindergarten?

a. she read it in the newspaper

b. a friend told her

c. the director has told her

7. Why did the director want to close the kindergarten?

a. because she was exhausted

b. because she had to move to another city

c. because she could not finance it anymore

8. What did Julia do?

a. She threw the newspaper away

b. She has sold her precious things

c. She sold her dog

9. Where did Julia go with the money?

a. to the doctor

b. to the director

c. in a bank

10. What happened in the end?

a. Julia got the job as an educator

b. the director has kicked her out

c. Julia bought a new car

Antworten

1. Sozialpädagogik

2. In einem Kindergarten

3. Mit der Direktorin

4. Weil sie keine Erfahrung hatte und die Direktorin meinte sie sei unreif

5. In den Park.

6. a

7. c

8. b

9. b

10. a

Answers

1. Social education

2. In a kindergarten

3. With the director

4. Because she had no experience and the director said she was immature

5. In the park.

6. a

7. c

8. b

9. b

10. a

Chapter 10 – Ein wahrer Held (A true hero)

Henry und Lucas waren zwei Jungs, die **nebeneinander** lebten. Als sie noch kleine Kinder waren, haben sie ständig zusammen gespielt und man kann sagen, dass sie sogar beste Freunde waren. Ihre Familien haben sich gut verstanden und waren sehr gute Nachbarn. Doch als die Jungs älter wurden und sie in die **Mittelschule** gehen mussten, haben sich die Dinge ein bisschen geändert. Henry war ein sehr intelligenter Junge und hatte in der Schule immer gute **Noten**, während Lucas einige neue Freunde fand, und die Schule als echte **Qual** empfand. Er hasste die Lehrer und fing an sich schlecht zu benehmen. Für ihn waren seine Freunde und die Partys am wichtigsten.

Henry and Lucas were two boys living side by side. When they were little kids, they played together all the time and you could say they were even best friends. Their families got along well and were very good neighbours. But as the boys got older and they had to go to middle school, things had changed a bit. Henry was a very smart boy and always got good grades at school, while Lucas made some new friends and for him school was a real torture. He hated the teachers and started behaving badly. For him, his friends and parties were most important.

Henry wusste, dass seine **Mitschüler** ihn nicht so sehr mogen. Die Lehrer liebten ihn aber. Dies war auch ein Grund, warum ihn seine **Klassenkameraden** ständig gemobbt haben. Sie machten Henry zum **Aussenseiter**. Die anderen würden ihm ständig neue **Spitznamen** geben und da Lucas seine Popularität nicht aufgeben wollte, hat er Henry auch **schikaniert**. Für Henry war dies aber kein Problem. Er wusste wer er ist und dass dies nicht seine Freunde waren. Er war ein wenig enttäuscht von Lucas, aber trotzdem hatte er seine **Ziele** im Kopf. Er wollte gut in der Schule sein und auch wenn ihn andere nicht akzeptierten, versuchte er ihnen bei **Prüfungen** zu helfen.

Henry knew his classmates did not like him so much. But the teachers loved him. That was one of the reasons his classmates bullied him constantly. They made Henry into a geek. The others would constantly give him new nicknames, and since Lucas did not want to give up his popularity, he bullied Henry as well. For Henry this was not a problem. He knew who he was and that these were not his friends. He was a little disappointed with Lucas, but still he had his goals in mind. He wanted to be good at school and even if others did not accept him, he tried to help them with exams.

Eines Tages kamen sie in die Klasse und Lucas stand vor all seinen Klassenkameraden und sagte:

One day they came to class and Lucas stood in front of all his classmates and said:

„Hey hört mal alle zu! Diesen Freitag habe ich das Haus für mich allein. Ich mach eine große Party und ihr sollt alle kommen. Es wird der Hammer, wie immer!"

"Hey, listen everyone! I have the house for myself this Friday. I'll have a big party and you should all come. It will be awesome, as always! "

Alle standen auf und gingen zu Lucas um sich über die Party zu freuen. Sie waren sehr aufgeregt und haben gelacht. Dann wollte Lucas noch etwas sagen:

Everyone got up and went to Lucas to talk about the party. They were very excited and laughed. Then Lucas wanted to say something else:

„Ich habe mich nicht sehr gut **ausgedrückt**. Alle können kommen, außer Henry. Sorry Mann, aber ich habe nicht so viel **Platz**, du weißt schon, oder?" Er lachte und **zwinkerte** seinen Freunden zu.

"I did not express myself very well. Everyone can come, except for Henry. Sorry man, but I do not have that much space, you know, right?" He laughed and winked at his friends.

Henry sah ihn für eine Sekunde an und drehte sich um, um seine Bücher rauszunehmen. Er war es schon gewohnt, dass keiner ihn zu Partys einladen wollte. Deswegen war er auch nicht **überrascht**. Alle lachten und haben ihn wieder **gemobbt**.

Henry looked at him for a second and turned to take out his books. He was used to not getting invited to parties. That's why he was not surprised. Everyone laughed and bullied him again.

Der Tag der Party kam an und alle waren aufgeregt und freuten sich. Henry ging nach der Schule nach Hause und spielte Videospiele. Er konnte schon am **Nachmittag** die laute Musik hören, aber er versuchte, sie zu ignorieren. Es war eine große Party und das Haus war voll.

The day of the party arrived and everyone was excited and happy. Henry went home after school and played video games. He could hear the loud music in the afternoon, but he tried to ignore it. It was a big party and the house was full.

In einem Moment, hörte Henry **Schreie** und laute **Geräusche**. Er stand aber nicht auf, denn er dachte, dass es nur laute Musik und Geschrei von der Party ist. Auf einmal hörte er aber etwas **merkwürdiges**.

In one moment, Henry heard screams and loud noises. He did not get up because he thought it was just loud music and screaming from the party. Suddenly, he heard something strange.

„Feuer!!!!!!! Oh mein Gott. Schnell!! Hilfeeee!!... FEUER!!" Diese Worte wiederholten sich ständig und alle haben geschrien.

"Fire!!!!!!! Oh my God. Fast!! Heeeelp !! ... FIRE !!" These words kept repeating and everyone was screaming.

Henry ging aus seinem Haus und sah ein Feuer auf dem zweiten Stock im Haus von Lucas. Er sah wie alle aus dem Haus ängstlich rannten. Henry rief die **Feuerwehr** gleich an. Alle waren draußen, doch er konnte Lucas nicht sehen.

Henry went out of his house and saw a fire on the second floor in Lucas's house. He saw how everyone in the house ran anxiously. Henry called the fire department immediately. Everyone was outside, but he could not see Lucas.

„Lucas ist im **Badezimmer** eingeschlossen. Er kann nicht raus! Hilfeee! Jemand muss ihn rausholen" – rief ein Mädchen aus der Masse.

"Lucas is trapped in the bathroom. He cannot get out! Heeelp! Someone has to get him out," a girl exclaimed from the crowd.

Henrys Herz klopfte nie schneller. Er musste etwas tun. Henry rannte schnell zu dem Haus und ging rein. Alle waren geschockt und waren in Panik. Er ging die **Treppe** auf und konnte nicht leicht atmen. Das Feuer hat sich schon überall ausgebreitet. Er musste die Tür des Badezimmers durchbrechen und danach ging er rein. Er sah Lucas auf dem Boden. Lucas konnte schwer atmen. Henry hebte ihn auf und versuchte Lucas aus dem Haus zu bringen. Es war sehr schwer aber er schaffte es bis zur Haustür. Alle waren geschockt als sie die beiden sahen. Zu dieser Zeit kam auch die Feuerwehr. Zum Glück konnten sie das Feuer schnell löschen. Ein **Feuerwehrmann** ging zu Henry und sagte:

Henry's heart never beat faster. He had to do something. Henry quickly ran to the house and went in. Everyone was shocked and in panic. He came upstairs and could not breathe easily. The fire was already everywhere. He had to break the door of the bathroom and then he went in. He saw Lucas on the floor. Lucas was breathing heavily. Henry lifted him and tried to get Lucas out of the house. It was very hard but he made it to the front door. Everyone was shocked when they saw them. At this time fire department arrived. Luckily they were able to extinguish the fire quickly. A fire-fighter went to Henry and said:

„Du bist ein sehr **mutiger** Junge. Ein wahrer Held. Du warst der einzige, der mutig genug war, um deinem Freund das Leben zu retten. Du hast dein eigenes riskiert. Das ist **unglaublich**."

"You are a very brave boy. A true hero. You were the only one brave enough to save your friend's life. You risked your own. That's incredible."

Henry antwortete:

Henry replied:

„Wir sind nicht Freunde, aber wir sind Menschen. Ich würde jedem helfen."

"We are not friends, but we are human. I would help everyone. "

Lucas war erschöpft aber er hat diese Worte gehört.

Lucas was exhausted but he heard those words.

„Henry, ich... ich kann es nicht glauben. Du hast mich gerettet. Wie habe ich das verdient." - fragte Lucas.

"Henry, I ... I cannot believe it. You saved me. How did I earn that?" asked Lucas.

„Du kennst mich Lucas. Auch wenn wir keine Freunde mehr sind, weist du immer noch, dass ich dir immer helfen würde." – antwortete Henry.

"You know me, Lucas. Even though we are no longer friends, you still know that I would always help you," replied Henry.

„Danke.. ich fühle mich so schlecht. Ich und die anderen haben dich immer gemobbt. Das war falsch. Am Ende warst du der einzige, der mich aus dem Feuer geholt hat...Glaubst du, dass wir wieder Freunde sein können? Ich verspreche dir, dass ich dich nie wieder enttäuschen werde. Ich werde nie zulassen, dass dir irgendjemand etwas schlechtes sagt...bitte..ich **vermisse** meinen besten Freund..."

"Thanks .. I feel so bad. Me and the others have always bullied you. That was wrong. In the end, you were the only one who got me out of the fire. Do you think we can be friends again? I promise you that I will never disappoint you again. I'll never let anyone tell you something bad ... please..I miss my best friend ... "

„Wir können es ja versuchen." – Henry zwinkerte und Lucas hatte wieder ein Lächeln auf seinem Gesicht.

"We can try it." Henry winked and Lucas had a smile on his face again.

Und es war auch so. Sie wurden wieder beste Freunde und alle anderen liebten Henry. Sie respektierten ihn für seine **Taten** und Henry war sehr **stolz** darauf.

And it was like that. They became best friends again and everyone else loved Henry. They respected him for his actions and Henry was very proud of it.

Zusammenfassung

Henry und Lucas waren früher beste Freunde und Nachbarn. Als sie in die Mittelschule kamen, änderte sich dies, weil Henry gemobbt wurde. Auch Lucas hat sich den anderen angeschlossen und mobbte Henry jeden Tag. Eines Tages hat Lucas eine Party in seinem Haus veranstaltet und hat alle eingeladen, außer Henry. Doch in einem Moment brach ein Feuer auf der Party aus und alle gingen nach draußen, außer Lucas. Er war im Badezimmer eingeschlossen. Henry hat die Schreie gehört und ging ins Haus. Er hat Lucas aus dem

Feuer geholt. Am Ende hat sich Lucas schlecht gefült, weil er Henry gemobbt hat, den er war der einzige, der ihm geholfen hat. Sie wurden danach wieder beste Freunde und alle anderen haben Henry für seine gute Tat respektiert.

Summary

Henry and Lucas used to be best friends and neighbours. When they entered middle school, it changed because Henry was bullied. Lucas also joined the others and bullied Henry every day. One day Lucas had a party in his house and he invited everyone but Henry. But in one moment a fire broke out at the party and everyone went outside, except for Lucas. He was trapped in the bathroom. Henry heard the screams and went into the house. He got Lucas out of the fire. In the end, Lucas felt bad because he bullied Henry, who was the only one who helped him. They then became best friends again and everyone else respected Henry for his good deed.

Wortschatz (Vocabulary)

nebeneinander – side by side

Mittelschule – middle school

Noten - grades

Qual - torture

Mitschüler - classmates

Klassenkameraden - classmates

Aussenseiter - outsider

Spitznamen - nickname

Schikaniert - bullied

Ziele - goals

Prüfungen - exams

ausgedrückt - expressed

Platz - space

zwinkerte - winked

überrascht - surprised

gemobbt - bullied

Nachmittag - afternoon

Schreie - screams

Geräusche - noises

Merkwürdiges - strange

Feuerwehr – fire department

Badezimmer - bathroom

Treppe - stairs

Feuerwehrmann - firefighter

mutig - brave

unglaublich - incredible

vermisse - miss

Taten - actions

Stolz – proud

Fragen

1. Was waren Lucas und Henry früher?

2. Warum haben die Mitschüler Henry gemobbt?

3. Worüber hat Lucas im Klassenzimmer gesprochen?

4. Wen hat Lucas nicht zur Party eingeladen?

5. An welchem Tag fand die Party statt?

6. Was hat Henry gehört?

a. Laute Musik und Schreie

b. Gekicher

c. Eine Gitarre

7. Was passierte auf der Party?

a. alle hatten Spaß

b. ein Feuer brach aus

c. Lucas war betrunken

8. Wo war Lucas als das Feuer ausbrach?

a. draußen

b. im Badezimmer

c. im Schlafzimmer

9. Wer hat Lucas gerettet?

a. der Feuerwehrmann

b. das Mädchen

c. Henry

10. Was passierte am Ende?

a. Lucas und Henry wurden wieder beste Freunde

b. Lucas hat Henry gemobbt

c. Henry war wütend

Questions

1. What were Lucas and Henry earlier?

2. Why did the classmates bully Henry?

3. What did Lucas talk about in the classroom?

4. Who did Lucas not invite to the party?

5. What day did the party take place?

6. What did Henry hear?

a. loud music and screams

b. laugh

c. a guitar

7. What happened at the party?

a. everyone had fun

b. a fire broke out

c. Lucas was drunk

8. Where was Lucas when the fire broke out?

a. outside

b. in the bathroom

c. in the bedroom

9. Who saved Lucas?

a. the firefighter

b. the girl

c. Henry

10. What happened in the end?

a. Lucas and Henry became best friends again

b. Lucas has bullied Henry

c. Henry was angry

Antworten

1. Beste Freunde

2. Weil er gute Noten hatte und die Lehrer ihn liebten

3. Über seine Party

4. Henry

5. Am Freitag

6.a

7.b

8. b

9. c

10. a

Answers

1. Best friends

2. Because he had good grades and the teachers loved him

3. About his party

4. Henry

5. On Friday

6. a

7. b

8. b

9. c

10. a

Conclusion

"Reading educates," they say. And in fact, through regular reading, the vocabulary expands automatically. The more often you are confronted with different words, the easier they become. By the way: if you read texts out loud, words are even easier to go from passive to active vocabulary. With half an hour of reading every day, you get a lot. Once that has become a habit, you will not want to miss it anymore. Why should you read more? The advantages are obvious: reading forms, reading extends your horizons, reading relaxes. And in addition, if you read in your learning language, you even have one more advantage: You learn the language and get a good feeling for sentence structure and vocabulary selection.

Perhaps the most obvious tip for more effective reading is unfortunately also difficult to implement. We all would like to read more, but in everyday life, it's hard to find time. To read every day, it has to become a regular habit. That's difficult at the beginning. Always carry this book with you. Read at a break, on the bus or while waiting for the bus. Also, having a regular time reserved for reading can help a lot. For example, you can read for half an hour every night before sleeping.

This is why we hope that you got all the advantages from reading the stories. You can always come back and read them over again. You'll see for yourself that it gets easier each time. Try to memorize and enjoy the interesting situations where the characters find themselves. Not only will you be better in German, but you'll learn some great life lessons through the stories. And don't forget: It takes time and patience, so don't force yourself and try to have fun while reading!

Preview of German
An Essential Guide to German Language Learning

Introduction

Whatever plans you may have for your future, with knowledge of the German language, you can create infinite possibilities. Learning German means acquiring skills to improve your professional and personal quality of life.

A global career: With German-language skills, you can improve your career prospects with German companies in your own country and in other countries. Good German skills make you a productive employee for an employer with global business relationships.

Tourism and hotel accommodation: Tourists from German-speaking countries travel far and wide, spending more on holiday than tourists from other countries. They are gladly introduced by German-speaking staff and German-speaking tour guides.

Science and research: German is the second most important language for science. With its contribution to research and development, Germany is third in the world in grant research fellowships to foreign scientists.

Communication: The developments in the media and information and communication technology require multilingual communication. A number of important websites are in German. Germany is ranked 6th in the world out of 87 countries, (just behind India, the UK, the USA, China and

Russia) in the annual production of new books. Your knowledge of the German language, therefore, allows you to access more information.

Cultural understanding: Learning German means gaining an insight into the life, the wishes, and the dreams of people in German-speaking countries, with their multicultural society.

Travel: With your knowledge of German, you can expand your travel experiences not only in the German-speaking countries, but also in other European countries, especially Eastern Europe.

Enjoyment of literature, music, art and philosophy: German is the language of Goethe, Kafka, Mozart, Bach and Beethoven. Speaking German allows you to deepen the enjoyment of reading and / or listening of their works in their original language.

Study and work opportunities in Germany: Germany awards a large number of scholarships to study there. There are special visas for young foreigners, and there are special provisions for work permits for certain professions.

Exchange programs: There are exchange programs between students from Germany and many countries around the world.

In business life: Communication in German with your German-speaking business partners leads to better business relations and thus to better opportunities for effective communication - and thus to success.

All these reasons and more are why learning German is a great idea. Start your journey with this amazing book!

Chapter 1 – Pronunciation

Learning the German alphabet

The basis of any language is its alphabet. It would be kind of embarrassing if you could speak a language, but you couldn't really spell your own name. In this chapter, you will have the opportunity to learn what you absolutely need to know about the German alphabet, and you will get answers to questions such as:

What is a "Umlaut?"

When to use "ß" and when "ss?"

How do you pronounce "sch" and "ch?"

The German alphabet has 26 letters, just like the English alphabet. In addition, there are the following "umlauts" (gray): Ü, Ö, Ä and the ß.

A, Ä, B, C, D, E, F, G, H, I, J, K, L, M, N, O, Ö, P, Q, R, S, ß, T, U, Ü, V, W, X, Y, Z

Alphabet with pronunciation A/a [a:]

Ä/ä [ɛ:]

B/b [be:]

C/c [tse:]

D/d [de:]

E/e [e:]

F/f [ɛf]

G/g [Ge]

H/h [HA]

I/i [i]

J/j [jɔt]

K/k [ka:]

L/l [ɛl]

M/m [ɛm]

N/n [ɛn]

O/o [o:]

Ö/ö [O]

P/p [pe:]

Q/q [ku:]

R/r [ɛr]

S/s [ɛs]

ß [ɛs'tsɛt]

T/t [te:]

U/u [u:]

Ü/ü [y:]

V/v [faʊ]

W/w [unit:]

X/x [ICS]

Y/y ['iupsilɔn]

Z / z [t͡sɛt]

Vowels

In the German alphabet there are 8 vowels.

A, E, I, O and U, and 3 Umlauts, Ä, Ü, Ö.

These are formed by two successive vowels:

Ü,ü   U+E (Bücher)

Ä, ä   A+E (Länder)

Ö,ö   O+E (Brötchen)

Diphthongs

Diphthongs are two consecutive vowels. "Ei" and "ai" sound the same, like "eu" and "äu." To figure out when to use which diphthong, it is helpful to form the word stem. "Mäuse (Mice)," for example, is formed from "Maus (Mouse)"; therefore the plural is formed with "au" instead of "eu." The diphthong "ei" is used much more frequently than the diphthong "ai" If you do not know which of the two to use, use the "ei," because the probability of getting it right is significantly higher. The "ie" is pronounced as a long "i." Again, it is difficult to know when it is a simple "I," and when it is an "ie."

Diphthong pronunciation examples:

EI/AI - as the English "I" - **I**ron/M**y**

IE – as the "e" in English – F**ee**l

EU/ÄU - similar to the "oi" in "to boil"

AU - similar to the "ou" in "to bounce"

Ss or β?

The ß (Esszett) is formed from a double "s"; it is a so-called "voiceless s." The Eßzett is used only after a long vowel, if one must consider whether one must use a double "s." For example, a sharp "s" is not used for "Lesen (read)" or "Rasen (lawn)." Unfortunately, there is no simple rule with which you can learn when to use the ß and when the ss. But the words with ß are limited. As long as you memorize them, you will be successful.

Here are a few common examples:

Spaß - fun

Straße - street

Gruß - greeting

Floß - raft

Heißen - be called

Groß - big

The "sch" and "ch"

The "ch" does not really exist in English. There are two different ways that Germans pronounce the "ch." The "sch" is almost always pronounced the same. The only exception is the letter sequence "ssch," which is pronounced as a double "s" and "ch" separated.

Ch - after "a, o, u, au" – in the back of the mouth – Bach

Ch - after "e, i, eu, ei, ä, ö, ü, äu, ai", or consonant like the "h" in "huge" – Fichte

Sch - always the same, (exception "ssch" (bisschen)) - like the "sh" in English

Letter case

German is not hard to learn. You just need to remember that all nouns and names are capitalized. Verbs and adjectives, as well as pronouns and conjugations, are lower case. As you have already noticed in this chapter, every word at the beginning of the sentence is capitalized after a point.

Summary

After completing this part, you should be able to spell your name. If a "ch" or "sch" occurs in your name, you now know how to pronounce it in German!

Exercises

1. Find and highlight the words containing "ch," which is pronounced like the "h" in "huge".

Heute Morgen bin ich um elf aufgewacht. Ich hatte Pech, denn ich habe den Wecker nicht gehört. Heute werde ich einfach zuHause bleiben. Vielleicht kann ich auch einen Film sehen. Es ist in Ordnung, wenn man sich ein bisschen von allem erholen will. Morgen ist wieder ein neuer Tag. Mein Vater holt mich ab und wir werden in einen Wald voller Fichten gehen. Vielleicht werden wir auch meine Schwester mitnehmen.

2. Insert the correct word from the parenthesis into the space.

a) _____ (Eulen/Äulen) sind sehr interessante Tiere.

b) Hier gibt es viele _____ (Heuser/Häuser).

c) Im _____ (Mei/Mai) hat _____ (meine/maine) Mutter Geburtstag.

d) Am Freitag _____ (flige/fliege) ich nach Italien.

e) Es ist wirklich _____ (heiß/haiß) draußen.

3. Insert the correct word.

a) Der _____ (Hund/hund) muss zum Tierarzt.

b) ___ (ich/Ich) bin sehr hungrig.

Hast du heute _____ (deine/Deine) Mutter gesehen?

c) Mein bester _____ (Freund/ freund) hat heute Geburtstag.

d) Hast du ____ (Lust/lust) mit mir spazieren zu gehen?

e) _____ (Heute/heute) ist ein sehr schöner Tag.

Chapter 2 – The basics

Nouns - main words

Mann, Hund, Katze, Maus: Nouns. In German, Nomen (nouns; also called "Hauptwort") is a word category. It refers to living beings, things, or facts. Nouns in German are always capitalized. In this chapter, you'll learn everything you need to know about nouns.

Why do I recognize the gender of a noun? That will determine which of the three common German articles (der, die, das) you have to use, which is a bit confusing for everyone who learns German as a foreign language.

How to form the plural of a noun? What is the plural of mouse? Mause or Mäuse?

What are the "4 cases" of the noun? And how do you recognize them?

After finishing this chapter, you should be able to answer all these questions!

Check out this book!

Printed in Great Britain
by Amazon